W9-AYI-413

JUNK

ENG

LISH

ALSO BY KEN SMITH

Mental Hygiene: Classroom Films 1945–1970

Raw Deal: Horrible and Ironic Stories of Forgotten Americans

Ken's Guide to the Bible

The New Roadside America
(coauthored with Doug Kirby
and Mike Wilkins)

JUNK ENGLISH

KEN SMITH

BLAST BOOKS NEW YORK

JUNK ENGLISH © 2001 Ken Smith

All rights reserved.

No part of this book may be reproduced in any form, by any means, without the express written consent of the publisher.

Blast Books gratefully acknowledges the generous help of Celia Fuller, Olga Gardner Galvin, Don Kennison, and Ken Siman.

Published by Blast Books, Inc.
P. O. Box 51, Cooper Station
New York, NY 10276-0051

ISBN 0-922233-23-3

DESIGNED BY LINDGREN/FULLER DESIGN

The text in this book is set in Janson.

Printed in the United States of America

First Edition 2001

10 9 8 7 6 5

For my parents, Anita and Herb

Language is the perfect instrument of empire.

—ANTONIO DE NEBRIJA,
BISHOP OF AVILA, 1492

CONTENTS

ACKNOWLEDGMENTS

This book could not have been written without the suggestions, support, and friendship of Michelle Boulé, Dorian Devins and Kevin Phelan, Don Faller and Toni DeMarco, Celia Fuller, Olga Gardner Galvin, Dotty Jenkins, Jamie Kelty, Don Kennison, Julie King, Doug and Susie Kirby, Jill Melamed, Litza Stark, Ken Swezey and Laura Lindgen, Mike Wilkins, and Dorothy Wilson.

A MESSAGE FROM KEN

Junk English takes many forms. It is the salesperson who describes a product as *high quality* and a *real value*, the coworker who writes of the *positive side of the consumer equation*, the politician who speaks of *sensible reform*, the television analyst who talks of *anomalous paradigms*, your best friend who says *Let's do lunch!*

All of us use junk English, often many times a day. That does not make it more forgivable, but more troubling.

Junk English is much more than sloppy grammar. It is a hash of human frailties and cultural license: spurning the language of the educated yet spawning its own pretentious words and phrases, favoring appearance over substance, broadness over precision, and loudness above all. It is sometimes innocent, sometimes lazy, sometimes well intended, but most often it is a trick we play on ourselves to make the unremarkable seem important. Its scope has been widened by politicians, business executives, and the PR and advertising industries in their employ, who use it to spread fog before facts they would rather keep hidden. The result is Edmund Burke's tyranny of the multitude merged with George Orwell's Newspeak, a world of humbug in which the more we read and hear, the less we know.

Junk English is the linguistic equivalent of junk food—ingest it long enough and your brain goes soft.

This book is a catalog of observations, not a text of grammar or style. I have salted it liberally with examples from everyday life. The errors and abuses are blatant and familiar; you will not need a degree in English to recognize them.

This book is also a broad overview of an encyclopedic subject. Much had to be pared away, particularly if it fell within wide-ranging topics such as Artificial Vocabulary, Euphemisms, and Jargon Gridlock. If your favorite atrocity is missing, I hope that you will understand. My intent was to keep this book small and handy so that it would be useful to a spectrum of people, for junk English will not go away until all of us recognize it.

This book is judgmental. Some may be uncomfortable with that. But we have been nonjudgmental for so long that abominations like *confab* and *smartize* and *impactful* and *conversating* have multiplied in our language and will continue to do so until we raise our hands in unison and say, "Pardon me, but what the hell does that mean?"

Junk English is not inevitable. We made it. We can make it go away. Thus this book.

All of the examples in this book (quoted without correction of typographical or grammatical error) were taken from life: newspaper and magazine articles; radio and television commentators; advertisements and editorials; minimum-wage workers and millionaire executives; the underclass and the ruling elite. None came from internal business or political memoranda; all were intended to be understood by ordinary people.

Abstract Adjectives. Adjectives are not frivolous. Their job is to describe the noun to which they are attached more fully and definitely: *desperate* author, *crazy* decision, *unread* book. Adjectives that are not definite are detrimental; if they do not make nouns clearer, they do not help others to understand what is being expressed.

Abstract adjectives in vogue are MAJOR, POSITIVE, QUALITY, and SERIOUS, with *alternative*, *feasible*, and IMPACT not far behind in popularity. Some of these are actually abstract nouns, and when paired as adjectives with other abstract nouns, e.g., *positive impact*, *serious alternative*, they make a great show but say little.

Address, when not used to describe the location of a building, is often employed by those who wish to be evasive and yet sound as if they are not.

Our product was specifically developed as a safe alternative for men who prefer an all-natural approach to address [treat] impotence.

I will address [confront] these policy issues.

Let me address [answer] that question.

"Any worthy energy policy must address [stop] the price gouging of consumers by greedy energy suppliers," Davis said.

Affordable is a word often used by advertisers who want to persuade buyers that a car or washing machine or bedroom set is inexpensive when it is not. An *affordable* product, sometimes inflated to *very affordable*, is one that a customer can fit within his or her budget, usually on the installment plan, with interest. Strictly speaking, the product is thus *affordable*, but *affordable* is not a synonym for *cheap*.

Ambiguity. The temptation to use words out of novelty or because they are fashionable is strong. This sometimes leads unwitting writers to create puzzling ambiguities.

The results of the cancer screening test were positive.

Most Silicon Valley insiders agree that the offering price is outrageous.

Should the recipient of the test results feel relieved or heartbroken? Is the stock being sold for a pittance or a fortune?

Anonymous Acronyms. Organizations engaged in politically or socially controversial activities sometimes compress their names, or the names of things within their domain, into a series of letters, in an attempt to mask the nature of their work. Thus the Consolidated Mining and Smelting Company of Canada becomes COMINCO, the Conservative News Service becomes CNS News, and Multi-Level Marketing—itself a EUPHEMISM for pyramid scams—becomes MLM. Sometimes this deception works and sometimes it doesn't.

Acronyms are meant to be easy to recall, the intent being that no one will need to refer to the lengthier phrase they stand for. The Geheime Staatspolizei (secret state police), for instance, reduced its name to the acronym GESTAPO, which was perhaps easier to recall than this organization ultimately wanted. Some modern acronym makers have learned to make their acronyms unpronounceable and innocuous. There is no chance that DWPF (Defense Waste Processing Facility) will ever roll lightly off the tongue or that MRM (Mechanically Recovered Meat) will ever call to mind a disagreeable image. Both are anonymous and easy to skip over, never even briefly tempting a reader to linger and think.

Apology words are special, earnest-sounding PARASITIC INTENSIFIERS, among them *genuinely, honestly*, 100%, *really, seriously, sincerely,* and *truly.* Their appearance tacitly concedes that the word or phrase that immediately follows has been stretched thin in current usage—*really* free, *sincerely* moved, *genuinely* shocked, *100%* legal—but that this time, honestly, what we are about to read is the truth.

> Would you seriously like to make $2,000–$5,000 per week starting right away?

> Take this opportunity to learn risk free the most effective way to truly meet that someone special.

> If you request removal we really will remove you immediately.

> This is honestly the most effective weight-reduction program I have ever tried.

Artificial Vocabulary. Everyone wants to sound smart, and many people seem to think the way to do that is to say ordinary things in extraordinary ways. An evening-news analyst thus speaks of a *paradigm* instead of a *model*, and a columnist writes of *recontextualization* rather than *rethinking.*

Although pretentiousness is usually offensive, sometimes something about a new word is appealing. When we hear someone say *mandate* instead of *goal*, or read in our morning paper of a *procedure* instead of a *task*, we may like the way it sounds and remember it, and the next time an opportunity arises to use it, we do. This is the viral nature of language in action.

There is nothing inherently wrong with polysyllabic or unusual words, as long as they are used correctly and appropriately. A word such as *interstitial* was not invented to impress but to convey a specific meaning, and those who breezily drop it into a sentence when all they mean to say is *filler* only call attention to their pretentiousness.

Popular artificial vocabulary includes *marginalize* for *weaken*, *expeditiously* for *quickly*, *a plethora of* for *many*, *gestalt* for *whole*, *persona* for *image*, *myopic* for *shortsighted*, *holistic* for *complete*, *dichotomy* for *difference*, *visage* for *face*. Words such as *virtually*, *aggregate*, *advocate*, and *documentation* have become so commonplace that one no longer even notices how they have usurped *almost*, *gather*, *urge*, and *paperwork*.

In a sense, the system we have designed to deal with offenders is among the most iatrogenic in history.

Some argue that the way Clinton left office has made the Bush presidency seem even more rectitudinous by contrast.

The software has opacity built into its codes.

The weather, dreary and gray, seemed a fitting denouement to this election year.

You will be invited to Oxford University for advanced tutelage.

Acting is not only about replicating life.

The President reavowed, with profound unction, that he shared "an ultimate dream" with the caucus members.

Aspect is a perfectly good noun to use when speaking of appearances or planetary phases, but it has for many years been incorrectly employed as a synonym for *part, portion,* and *share.* This has gone on long enough that it now sounds correct to many.

> Economics was only one aspect of Gore's campaign strategy, but an important aspect intermingled with other elements.

> What are the educational aspects of this decision?

Assure and **Ensure**. One *assures* something—*You are safe, I assure you*—but is *ensured* of something—*He worked hard to ensure his victory. Assure* is frequently used in places where *ensure* would have been the appropriate word.

> Our vision for the future is to elevate performance standards to assure continued success.

> Look for the Energy Star label to assure that you're purchasing products that are energy efficient.

> Everything we serve must meet the exceptionally high standards of our rigorous quality assurance program.

The freakish term *quality assurance* has become popular, perhaps because *quality ensurance* is difficult to pronounce. An earlier term, *quality control,* seems to have been forgotten.

Bad connections, similar in awkwardness to OBESE PREPOSITIONS and THE ROUNDABOUT WAY, are phrases we encounter every day and probably think little of, but they add immeasurably to the bulk and feebleness of modern English. They link one part of a sentence to another, but they do it cumbrously, with a lumbering train of prepositions, passive verbs, and abstract nouns, replacing what otherwise could be expressed in a word or two.

A bad connection in English, like its counterpart in life, calls attention to itself when all one wants is a clear line from A to B. A few can be trimmed to single words—*within* [the framework of], *is* [representative of], [the question as to] *whether.* Bad connections number into the thousands.

make an appearance with	appear with
is capable of being	can be
tasked with the job of	chosen to
continuing with this example	to continue
has become enamored of	enjoys
is dedicated to providing	provides
specializes in providing	provides
in the event that	if

with a view to	intending to
direct your attention to	look at, read
it remains to be seen whether	it may or may not
it is imperative that we	we must
is highly dependent on	requires
is at the forefront of providing	offers
brought about the organization of	organized
it is likely that	probably
in certain/some instances	sometimes
significantly expedite the process of	speed
at which time	then
in the final analysis	ultimately
is committed to	wants
is focused on	wants
at such time	when

Battlefield Language. The business world has embraced the language of warfare as its primary source of metaphor. Fierce and often brutal English is dispatched from corporate boardrooms every day and enthusiastically reported by the business press, all for the purpose of announcing what so-and-so company intends to do with such-and-such product. It is declared, for example, that the *upper echelon* of company A plans to *battle* the competition and *capture* market share with a *barrage* of advertising, while company B is *spearheading* a drive with new sales *tactics* and an *escalating* price *war* in *target* markets while *mobilizing allied* companies to avoid *liquidating* inventory, and that the primary objective of company C is to *roll out* breakthrough products and *deploy* its sales *force strategically* to meet *mission-critical* goals in its *domain*. All three companies, without question, will *engage* in income tax *maneuvers*.

The often-violent metaphors of battlefield language are unsettling when they appear outside the context of business.

> The vast majority of the public welcomes anything they can utilize to make their visit safer and do a preemptive strike on crime.

> Lee's memory for individual artist styles is the most valued weapon in her arsenal.

> The show is targeted at 18-to-24-year-olds.

Black is white is an approach taken by some advertisers in which what is stated, clearly and boldly, is the exact opposite of what is true.

The theory behind it, popular among propagandists, is that people are more apt to believe a big lie than a little one, and that where one lie is good, two and sometimes three are even better.

> Let us give you the facts so you can make an educated decision.

> This material is for informational purposes only and should not be construed as an offer or solicitation of an offer to buy.

> This is not a get-rich quick scheme.

> Here's proof.

Your financial dreams are an absolute reality with this complete package.

THIS IS DIFFERENT THEN ANYTHING ELSE YOU'VE SEEN!

Business jargon is anything but businesslike. Those who use it cavalierly turn verbs into nouns and nouns into adjectives, bandy about unpronounceable acronyms and technical terms, and invent slang at a rate that would put a teenager to shame.

Although jargon often sounds ugly to outsiders, it speeds communication within the community that uses it. Those on the outside have no cause to protest, for example, when an internal publication of the post office reports that *If an OCR could be installed in front of each AFCS, the need for manual facing could be dramatically reduced*, or when a telecommunications journal informs its readers that *The industry can soon expect vendors to start delivering interoperable switches based on the FC-SW2 standard*. For its audience this language is both proper and clear.

But there is another kind of business jargon that is nothing but pretentious lingo. This ranges from overblown words such as *conceptualize* and *functionality*, to long-winded names for ordinary things such as *capitalized cost reduction* [down payment] and *objective baseline indicators* [guidelines], to nearly incomprehensible verb-adjective-noun abominations such as *synergize seamless iterations* and *transition holistic deliverables*. Businesspeople have always had a weakness for this kind of talk, and its modern-day flourishing is a natural result of the desire to make ordinary jobs seem special, and of the popular media's remaking of the business world into something not merely about making money but something chic.

Business jargon has become common parlance in news reports on topics that are not about business. To write of *the return on investment* [profit] we can expect from our Middle East policy or of the *net positive impact* [improvement] in our policing of environmental laws, or to talk of the need for *better cash flow management* [less reckless spending] in the average American home is to reduce matters of politics, environmental protection, and family to mere dollars and cents.

Capital Offenses. The humble written word—letters on a page or computer screen—is ill-equipped to grab our attention in an age of hype and stimulation. Advertising agencies determined to raise our temperature to the buying point are left with few choices. Lacking the means to write with sufficient vigor and clarity, they choose instead to manipulate their words graphically: they set the type large or small, tack on exclamation marks (sometimes even two or three), and use color, italics, boldface, or, most popular of all, capitalization. The power of capitalizing a word lies in its implied message: the word must be important.

Capitalizing escalates quickly as each copywriter feels impelled to outshout the competition, leading, ultimately, to overuse that renders capitals pointless.

Would you and your family Enjoy a better life if you knew how to get out of Debt?

This Proven, Almost Secret Method was Discovered Over 10 Years Ago By A Group Of Attorneys in Florida And California, For Creating New Credit Files Has Been Used successfully By Thousands of Americans Just Like YOU!

There are only 2 situations left here. You don't try the system, convincing yourself that this is just another empty promise and it won't work. Because you don't believe it will, you don't even try it, and your FINANCIAL SITUATION STAYS THE SAME . . . OR- YOU FOLLOW THE GLIMMER OF HOPE THAT IS SPARKED IN YOU RIGHT NOW, MAKE THE DECISION TO TRY IT, TAKE THE ACTION, AND ONE DAY REALIZE WHEN YOU ARE COLLECTING INCOME FROM YOUR MAILBOX, THAT YOU ALMOST DIDN'T EVEN TRY THIS!!!

The popularity of e-mail has led to a new problem with capitalized words—the absence of them. Those who write e-mail this way are perhaps trying to make as seamless as possible the connection between thought and expression, with a speed that cannot allow for the depression of the shift key. An extreme example:

Hey listen Tom i just want to say i think your a moron we have a serious readiness crisis in this countries military and we need to counter we need to increase the budget for military spending and we need to do it now obviously you dont know anything about the military or the type of threats our country faces and thats a shame because a man in your position shouldnt go around pretending like he knows everything but when we dont have a missile defense system and your family gets vaporized dont come crying to me cause your sorry you dint see need for it

Cheapened Words. Unlike OVERWORKED EMPHASIZERS, which have always had the job of intensification, cheapened words were originally used as justified descriptions of rare, exceptional attributes or conditions. There's nothing wrong with describing the rise of Joan of Arc as a *miracle*, the Eiffel Tower *unique*, Leonardo da Vinci's *Last Supper* a *masterpiece*, the discovery of penicillin a *breakthrough*, Tchaikovsky's *1812 Overture* a *classic*. But these special words, and others of similar stature, are now being attached to unworthy subjects.

Business, especially, has of late been burning out formerly exclusive words in a firestorm of hyperbole. When every executive is a *visionary*, every product *revolutionary*, every instance of mismanagement a *crisis*, every idea *innovative*, every unsolicited offer *exclusive*, by what names will we know the true articles when they come along? *Megarevolutionary*? *Supercrisis*? *Extraexclusive*? Elevation of the mundane and mediocre leaves us unable to identify excellence or incompetence, which perhaps is the point.

Some writers have tried to cheat by describing products as *revolutionary in nature*. It does not work.

Clichés are the many thousands of stale metaphors and phrases enlisted as poor excuses for expression. Among the most popular nowadays are *on the same page*, *the net result*, *outside the box*, *pushing the envelope*, and *a win-win situation*.

A frequent trick among those who resort to clichés is to spike them with extra adjectives in an attempt to add zest:

> The only cloud on the immediate horizon is that many markets report an anticipated increase in sublease space.

The 46-year-old constitutional lawyer does not cut the kind of abrasive figure that her controversial mentor, James Watt, did.

There is nothing wrong with putting one's best fashion foot forward.

The group cut their electronic teeth on their first album.

Writers also occasionally change a word or two in a cliché, modifying it to suit the purpose at hand. When a cliché does not express what you want to say, swapping in different words will not make it better.

However, there is a kernel of usefulness [truth] to what the WTO members will discuss among themselves later this month.

Given the generally disreputable nature of the folks on the presidential pardon list, this apparent deal may be just the tip of the scandal [iceberg].

Clichés, although popular objects of scorn, are useful when they most succinctly express an idea; deliberate avoidance of an appropriate cliché sometimes produces even worse writing.

Community is a useful word meaning *a gathering together of similar things* (nations, people, insects, etc.). It has, however, been much in fashion recently as SOCIAL WELFARE LINGO, used as a trendy substitute for *local*. Its appearance in a phrase such as *International, National, and Community Affairs* ignores the logical sequence of the phrase.

Community is also often used as a SECRET SNOB WORD in phrases such as *health care community, teaching community*, etc. Calling people employed in certain professions a *community* instead of *workers* is lexicon elitism. In a society that supposedly thumbs its nose at pretensions, we say *medical community* and *legal community*, but *sanitation workers* and *construction workers*.

Complimentary. The word *complimentary*, when applied to something given to someone, means that it is given as a courtesy or favor. The word has been misused for so long as a substitute for FREE that most people have forgotten about the business of courtesy. Unsolicited, so-called complimentary issues of magazines, for example, are never given as a courtesy or favor but as an enticement to subscribe. Bait, yes; free, yes, in a way; complimentary, no.

Convenience, like OPPORTUNITY, is a word of substance that has been devalued by those with something to sell. It is now just another EUPHEMISM for *product* or *service*.

> Announcing a new convenience for our cardmembers—the power to send and receive money by e-mail.

Cynic incubators are words and phrases that the politically minded have embraced as tools to further particular agendas.

Generations of politicians have manipulated certain words, turning them into cynic incubators: *balance, benefit, bold, clean,*

democratic, fair, freedom, improve, liberty, logical, MODERATE, OPPOR-
TUNITY, *order, progress, realistic, reasonable,* REFORM, *responsible, safe,
sane, sensible, truth.* Those used negatively include *disastrous,* DRA-
CONIAN, *extreme, irresponsible, radical, reckless,* and *waste* (more can
be found under SMEARS). POSITIVE, a weak adjective, is often set to
work as a cynic incubator. Had Hitler lived today, he would no
doubt have characterized the establishment of Auschwitz as "A
positive step on the road to the solution of the Jewish issue."

Cynicism blossoms when one discovers, for example, that an
organization with the unarguably benevolent-sounding name the
Progress and Freedom Foundation is in fact a business-bankrolled
Washington, D.C., group that advocates government sale of the
electromagnetic spectrum to private corporations; or that the
National Endangered Species Act Reform Coalition was put
together by electric utility companies to hamstring the Endangered Species Act; or that the American Council on Science and
Health is funded by Burger King, Coca-Cola, PepsiCo, Nutra-
Sweet, Nestlé USA, Monsanto, Dow USA, Exxon, Union Car-
bide, and others, and has claimed that the government spends too
much money investigating dioxin and pesticides, defends the
safety of saccharin and of growth hormones for dairy cows, and
reports that eating Whoppers is not as unhealthy as we have
been led to believe.

Cynic incubators are one of the principal tools with which
public-relations firms ply their trade. A small sample of their
grim work follows: names of industry-funded "political action
committees" (pressure groups) and "advocacy organizations"
(soft-money distributors) that have been draped in fair-minded
titles to hide their bias.

Civic Involvement Program of General Motors Corporation

Constructive Citizenship Program of Texas Instruments

Fisher Scientific International Inc. Employees Committee for Sensible Government

Loral Spacecom Civic Responsibility Fund

Mead Corporation Effective Citizenship Fund

Pennsylvania Power & Light Co. People for Good Government

Pepsico Inc. Concerned Citizens Fund

United Brotherhood of Carpenters & Joiners of America Legislative Improvement Committee

Cynical. Otherwise perceptive writers and speakers have fallen into the trap of abusing *cynical*, a SMEAR word frequently employed by politicians and product-pushers to tarnish those who doubt their claims. Many have apparently forgotten the words *wary*, *skeptical*, *cautious*, and *suspicious*, less pejorative than *cynical* and more precise in most cases.

The young are cynical [skeptical] about politics and so have withdrawn from the system.

She was more cynical about [wary of] the police than her mother because of what she'd seen.

Deal with is a term made popular as SELF-HELP JARGON and now firmly established in American idiom.

It's your problem; deal with it.

Ever wonder how you would deal with the kinds of situations that only come up when you are a movie action hero?

How Bush will deal with the Democrats, still smarting from their election losses, will be of interest to more than one EU foreign office.

Deal at has become the illiterate way to say *work with* or *report to.*

All of my clients are Fortune 500 companies. I deal at the executive level.

I'm either dealing at the chief executive officer, or the chief operating officer level.

The Default Dozen. Computers and other electronic devices come with factory default settings, which are what we use to operate the equipment if we neglect to change them. Similarly the default dozen are twelve words that come to mind automatically when we neglect to think of better ways to say what we mean.

They are: FACTOR, focus, FUNCTION, IMPACT, ISSUE, LEVEL, MAJOR, POSITIVE, PROCESS, QUALITY, SERIOUS, and SIGNIFICANT, with *major, positive, serious,* and *significant* acting as ABSTRACT ADJECTIVES to the abstract nouns in the dozen and *quality* serving as both. The particular horror of the default dozen is that their territory has expanded so rapidly, escaping the boardroom and Washington beltway breeding grounds to infest everyday speech. People now commonly talk about the *process* of organizing a child's birthday party, or of the *factors* that went into determining a vacation destination, or of wanting a *quality* personal relationship, or of taking an existing relationship to the next *level.*

Deserve, like HASSLE-FREE, is used in advertising pitches to appeal to people who feel abused by life, the system, or whatever they choose to blame. *You deserve a break today* was a great success for McDonald's for this reason; today's appeals to the downtrodden follow a similar pattern.

> Put yourself in control of the credit you deserve.
>
> If you have a faulty joint or hip replacement you may deserve a big cash settlement.

Get MULTIPLE OFFERS and get the loan you
want...and DESERVE!

Imagine the feeling you'll have knowing that you have the
money to buy what you want! Well, why not? Don't you
deserve it? You most certainly do!

The word *earn* is similarly used, as in *At this stage in your life
you've earned a little luxury.*

Desexed Designations. The drive for equal rights for women
has produced numerous inventive recastings of formerly sex-
specific job designations. *Musician, lawyer, doctor, teacher, banker,
minister, mechanic, astronaut,* and *librarian* are occupational descriptions that are intrinsically neutral. Others, however, have
required manipulation, mostly to avoid the necessity of applying
the desexed designations *-people* or *-persons*, both loudly decried
at first for the graceless words that resulted. Of the formerly
common sex-specific designations, only *businessmen* and *salesmen*
are now *-persons* and *-people* in regular usage. Sportsmen became
athletes; firemen, *firefighters;* policemen, *police officers;* mailmen,
postal workers; garbagemen, *sanitation workers;* and stewardesses,
flight attendants—the latter two complete shifts to EUPHEMISMS.
Milkmen largely ceased to exist, conveniently eliminating the
need for a name change.

One curious example of a desexed designation is *con artist* (or
scam artist), which replaced *con man* or *confidence man,* thus making
swindling the only occupation that went sexless and received an
elevation of status into the bargain. If it is the skills of an artist that
are required to talk people out of their money, why not *sales artist*

instead of *salesperson*? Or if *conperson* is too clumsy, why do we have no problem replacing *craftsman* with *craftsperson*? Ironically, most con artists as they are popularly defined—the smooth talker who wants to cheat you in an investment scam—*are* men; in fact, not being subject to equal opportunity laws, con artistry is probably one of the most male-dominated professions in the country.

Dialogue is a SELF-HELP JARGON word and is used as a substitute for *discussion*, even in instances where *discussion* would be more appropriate.

> Bush should get together with black people with whom he could get into a fruitful dialogue on the effects of racial profiling.

Dialogue has been given this job because *discuss* is now thought to imply dissatisfaction. Perhaps the phrase *We need to discuss this* is responsible, although *discuss* here is actually an impartial word trapped in a euphemistic role—a way to say *I'm going to tell you why I think you're wrong.*

Distraction modifiers are effective because of SELF-DECEPTION. They include the words *a low*, JUST, and *only*, placed, for example, before an unappealing number.

> Save with a low 12.9% fixed rate.

> You can obtain a complete one-month supply for just $69.95.

Other distraction modifiers are the words *easy, merely,* and *simply,* placed before an unpleasant activity.

> Twelve easy monthly payments.

> Simply fill in and mail back the attached order card.

The use of the word *partial* in the phrase *partial meltdown* is an example of just how far this approach can be pushed.

Distraction modifiers are the opposite of INVISIBLE DIMINISH-ERS, although, paradoxically, they operate on the same principle.

Do is a tiny but voracious cannibal; legions of verbs have disappeared into its maw and the big feed isn't likely to end any time soon. Brevity and euphony allow *do*'s casual—some would say sloppy—use as the language's all-purpose verb, and we like it for that reason. Grammarians may cringe at *What do you do?* but it sounds better than *What is your profession?*

Do is always understood in context or is at least never questioned. When a young man whispers to his partner, "Let's do it," or when a mother scolds her child, "Don't do that," the coy response is always "Do what?" never "What do you mean by 'do'?"

Do is unnecessary when used in efforts to be obsequious—*We do hope this incident was not an inconvenience to you*—and modern idiom awkwardly substitutes it for a range of words, quietly eradicating others from our vocabulary.

> This is a quick and easy system that anyone can do [learn].

> We do [cook] chicken better!

A collection of animal escape stories would be something I'd love to do [write].

Let's do lunch. [Let's have lunch together.]

Downside and **upside** are creatures of Wall Street, succinct ways of saying that an investment has a chance to lose or make money, as in *This stock has low potential downside.* If left to the brokers and fund managers, these words would be inoffensive and useful, but they have infiltrated general usage.

The upside of the discussions was that the two sides agreed in principle to a cease-fire.

The signers want to stimulate a national dialogue about the potential downsides of estate tax repeal.

Downturn and *upturn* have remained within the vernacular of finance but are frequently misused in place of *fall* and *rise*. *Downturn* and *upturn* should be used only when something reverses direction; to say *the market continued its downturn* is nonsense.

Draconian. Commentators have long been in love with *draconian*. It sounds impressive, much more ominous and foreboding than *rigorous, stern, severe, harsh*, or even *cruel*. Those who resort to this word are also signaling that their opinion is not one of dispassionate observation.

Basically, the government is "hog tying" the American people in all sorts of draconian laws that they can enforce selectively and at will.

The term *draconian measures* is also favored among those who find *unprecedented power* or *overwhelming power* not draconian enough for their tastes.

Remember the Omnibus Crime Bill passed in the late 1990s? It put draconian measures in the hands of the police and took our civil rights away.

Ear. Most people write to some extent by ear. Having an ear for what works and what does not is vital to fine writing, even more fundamentally so than memorizing rules of grammar. Developing that ear, however, has grown difficult as those who are in the business of communicating ideas nowadays are often political double-talkers and salespeople. Our ear has consequently become accustomed to hundreds of empty phrases and bloated words such as *the fact of the matter is, functionality,* and *on a daily basis.* To read these and believe that they sound impressive and intelligent is to be a casualty of those who would rather not distinguish good English from bad, and who would have us become similarly undiscerning.

Educate. The word *teach* is gradually being retired in favor of *educate*, as in *The executive director wants to educate prisoners about how to navigate the system when they come up for parole.* In another example, a group of Kansas teachers recently decided *teachers* no longer accurately described their occupation, and after much debate they chose a new term, *educational facilitators.* The creation of this ponderous synonym, SOCIAL WELFARE LINGO at its worst, was not an exercise in self-love; it was an earnest attempt at precision, as the teachers felt that *teacher* implied someone who simply delivers information, while their new title made clear, in their minds, their goal of helping young people to help themselves.

The teachers' new title did not solve their problem; it merely replaced an understandable two-syllable word with a hazy ten-syllable term. Their intent was honorable; their execution was atrocious. Perhaps *thought-enablers* or *thought-helpers* would have done as well (if as awkwardly), or perhaps they needed someone simply to stand up and say that a person who teaches someone to teach themselves is still a teacher.

Curiously, the adjective *educational* is being pushed aside by *informational*, as in *informational seminar*. The effect is limitation: *informational* promises the mere delivery of facts, whereas *educational* implies being given information and the intellectual means to use it. Since the two words look similar, *informational* has the double benefit to its users of offering less while appearing not to.

Effect is commonly misused as a nucleus around which feeble verb phrases cluster, to avoid describing specific damage to or disease of the human body. IMPACT sometimes fills this role as well.

> Cortisone, in addition to its effect on [harming] the nervous system, has a negative impact on [injures] muscle and bone.

The terms *health effects* and *health concerns* also often replace the names of specific diseases. Many journalists in print and electronic media are content to call radiation damage to the human body *severe health effects* instead of *burns, nausea, cancer,* and *death,* and describe the wasting illness caused by smoking as *long-term health effects* instead of as *cancer, emphysema,* and *heart disease.*

Social effects is often seen as a EUPHEMISM for *social disruption,* but the pliability of the phrase defies easy definition, a desirable attribute for the writers and politicians who use it.

> The social effects of continued Ecstasy use among young people have yet to be measured, but early indications are troubling.

> As far as voting on the Internet is concerned, it should not be allowed. Significant questions remain as to security, reliability, and the social effects.

Euphemisms are mild words or colorless expressions used to camouflage disagreeable truths. They are a tool of propaganda and have had a long, tarnished career in the service of diplomats, elected officials, and other purveyors of legitimized dishonesty. The Nazis, although far from the first government to use pleasant-sounding words to hide unpleasant facts, lowered this cynical art to depths rarely equaled: *special treatment* was hanging; *resettlement* was forced deportation to concentration camps or sometimes simply mass murder. In framing our own Constitution, men such as Thomas Jefferson and George Washington deliberately substituted *migration* and *importation* for *the slave trade,* while southern politicians of the nineteenth century used the affable term *our peculiar institution* to avoid saying *slavery.*

Ironically, the more successful a euphemism is, the less effective it becomes. *Pre-owned*, for example, is a euphemism created in the 1960s that has enabled luxury-car dealers and used Rolex watch salespeople to charge more for secondhand goods. It has become so ingrained in American idiom that many no longer recognize it as a euphemism; *pre-owned* is accepted as a natural synonym for the word it was supposed to make us forget.

Business, which has embraced many nasty methods of political language, has developed a ravenous appetite for euphemisms. The impressive volume of business euphemisms entering the language leads one to imagine meetings, hundreds a day, in which the creation of a euphemism to hide intentions and make the unsavory look appetizing is the sole expression of creativity.

accept this special invitation = pay money
build relationships = get money from
cold pasteurization = irradiation
competitive intelligence = business spying
convenience fee = interest charge
cooperative marketing = pyramid scam
[stock market] *correction* = crash
customer care representative = telemarketer
downsized = laid off
e-mail marketing = junk e-mail
floor assistant = salesperson
gaming = gambling
a high element of risk = a good chance you'll lose your money
innovator medicine = brand-name drug
introduce = sell (*Use e-mail to introduce your product or service.*)
invest = gamble

investigational medication = experimental drug

marketing offers = junk mail, telemarketing calls (*You will receive marketing offers by telephone and mail.*)

misdeeds = crimes

money factor = finance charge

multilevel business = pyramid scam

multilevel business partners = suckers

multilevel marketing = pyramid scam

network marketing = pyramid scam

processing (of animals) = slaughtering, killing

product specialist = salesperson

relationship manager = salesperson

security service = armed guard

share = sell (*I understand that you may share this information with other interested businesses.*)

sources = informants (*inside sources*)

special criteria = restrictions

streamlined = laid off

terminate = fire

unauthorized = illegal (*We'll alert you to any possible unauthorized card use.*)

underutilized = not exploited enough (*According to western lawmakers, public lands are underutilized.*)

uneconomical = unprofitable (*This change in your terms is due to our determination that current pricing is uneconomical.*)

unfortunate = wrong, lies (*Mr. Bush's comments are unfortunate.*)

urban unrest = riots

work stoppage = strike, lockout

Using euphemisms to avoid straightforward English can reach absurd extremes. *When the Human Waste Management Plant No Longer Functions*, for example, is the title of a class in which EMS paramedics learn to treat patients with kidney failure.

Experience has long been abused as a pretentious synonym for *feel*, as when an advertisement invites one to experience the creaminess of ice cream, the silkiness of pantyhose, the power of a V-8 engine. Advertising writers have found new uses for this impressive-looking word, using it as a substitute for *trip*, as in *This is a unique wilderness river experience for everyone!*; or *enjoy*, as in *Experience the fun of Disney World this holiday season;* or tacking it arbitrarily onto unexciting activities to give them a sense of importance.

Call our Customer Care Center to comment on your flight experience.

We've turned around the car buying experience.

The best luxury shopping experience on the planet!

Event is similarly misused, as in *The most controversial television movie event of the year!*

Extra words litter hundreds of idiomatic American expressions. Often they are redundant, as is *together* in *bond together;* sometimes they are absurd, as is *diverse* in *diverse cross section;* and sometimes they are habitual, as is *theoretically* in *theoretically possible.*

But they are always space-wasters, adding no information or shade
of meaning.

(any and) all (*Any and all information is kept strictly confidential.*)
anything (at all)
begins (promptly)
career (path)
collect (together)
(completely) surrounded
(conclusive) proof
(contained) in
(core) audience, market, values
(custom) tailored
delegate (responsibility)
dollar (amount) (*rounded to the nearest dollar amount*)
(end) result
every (last) one
a few (short) years
(general) public (*This is the first time that the general public has
    been given the opportunity to determine the content of a Super
    Bowl commercial.*)
(information) report
knowledge (base) (*This revelation adds to our knowledge base.*)
(live) operator (*Should you not reach a live operator please leave
    your name and phone number.*)
(located) in, on (*Simply call the toll-free number located on the
    front of your bill.*)
mixed (together)
now (currently)

on (the face of the) earth (*Americans are the most wasteful people on the face of the earth.*)

own (personal)

(period of, point in) time (*a very short period of time*)

(personal) opinion

(planned) strategy

(purchase) price

risk (factor)

(separate) pieces (*The company owns 152 separate pieces of property.*)

(specific) details

staff (count) (*CNN is reducing its total staff count from 4,350 to 3,950.*)

stressed (out)

those (persons) named

time (frame, period, scale) (*Our ability to assist you may be lessened if we do not receive your letter within this time frame.*)

(usual) habits

(victory) win (*Last year he finished in the top sixteen. This was his first victory win.*)

weather (conditions)

Facilitate has been embraced by those who like its sound, who believe it makes them appear smart and important, and who overuse it to the point where it irritates people who remember when we used to say *Let's make this easier* rather than *Let's facilitate this*. Worse, it is often used as a synonym for words to which it has no relation.

Our monthly pricing method is intended to facilitate [broaden] customer choice by keeping our commodity charges closer to competitive market prices.

Copper facilitates [builds] connective tissue and promotes bone development.

Sometimes the desire to use *facilitate* is so strong that a writer will insert it where it is unnecessary, apparently only for show.

They aren't far from being a contender again, if they can keep the current team together. They hope a new stadium would help facilitate that.

Facilitator owes its overuse to the current fashion for SELF-HELP JARGON. It is the good twin of *enabler*, with none of that word's pejorative connotations, and provides a way to make what used to be called a *manager* or *engineer* or, as a metaphor, *shepherd*, sound more important.

Fact. It is sad—there is no other word for it—that *fact* has become a popular word with the dishonest and long-winded. Its employment as an opposite of its meaning is covered under BLACK IS WHITE. When used as part of a BAD CONNECTION, *fact* and its accompanying phrase can always be replaced by a simple preposition or conjunction. *In spite of the fact that* can be reduced to *although*; and *due to the fact that, in view of the fact that*, and *owing to the fact that* can be replaced by *as, since*, or *because*.

The most common abuse of all, *the fact that*, frequently can be shortened to the simple *that*.

> What makes this kind of advertising so effective is the fact that it goes right to the potential customer.

In most common uses, *fact* and its accompanying phrase can simply be deleted.

> The term "Potemkin village" has become a metaphor for things that look impressive but in actual fact lack substance.

Fact is often incorporated into stalling phrases that tell readers or listeners only that something is about to be said.

[It is a fact of life that] the ratings numbers for virtually everything on network television are down.

[Part of this misconception stems from the fact that] many people have trouble thinking of gambling as an addiction at all.

Factor is the most frequently overused, misused, abused word in today's junk English lexicon.

There was a time when Washington was intimidating for me. You have to get over that mental factor [hurdle].

That's definitely a factor [important].

A few factors [conclusions] seem obvious on the eve of the Superbowl, factors [conclusions] all tied to the ratings.

Sometimes a writer, perhaps aware of the overuse of *factor*, uses ARTIFICIAL VOCABULARY and makes matters worse.

For many growing enterprises at that time, cheaper land and more fluid transportation were the key desiderata.

Fat-ass Phrases. Once recognized, fat-ass phrases reveal their bulk readily. At the end of each fat-ass phrase drags an abstract noun: *alternative*, *arena*, *basis*, *character*, *concept*, EFFECT, *effort*, EXPERIENCE, *fashion*, LEVEL, *manner*, MODE, *nature*, *plane*, PROCESS, *prospect*, QUALITY, SITUATION, *thing*—a warning signal that bloating is present.

Clinton entered the political arena [politics] at an early age.

The withholding concept [Withholding] is often poorly understood.

He had a brash character [was brash].

I would like to thank the many people who made this past year such a rewarding experience [so rewarding].

Growth is slow in the meatpacking sector [meatpacking].

You need to exercise on a daily basis [daily].

It's almost a spiritual thing [spiritual].

Feel or **Think**? There is a hesitancy to use the word *think* in modern American English. Thinking, when it must be referred to, is transformed into the pretentious *thought process. What was the thought process that led to this decision?* The oblique *take it under consideration* has replaced *think about it*, while *think* is avoided by using *feel* or *believe*, as in, *We feel there is a very substantial potential for growth.*

In advertising copy *think* appears only when one is asked *not* to think, to take a leap of faith, e.g., *Think of the possibilities. Think for a moment. Dare to think where you could be one year from now.*

Feel, aside from serving as a replacement for *think*, appears to have fallen out of favor in popular writing, sometimes to the point of absurdity.

Perfect for Valentine's Day or any occasion, flowers can really express your sentiment [feelings].

First class, applied to a product or service, is gradually being replaced by the terms *world class, best-in-class, top of the class, top shelf, first quality, five star,* and *the gold standard.* First-class hotel rooms are now known as *superior* or *grand* rooms, and airlines are replacing the term with euphemistic names such as *executive class* and *connoisseur class,* although one British carrier has renamed its first class *upper class* in a tongue-in-cheek swipe at English social stratification. (The use of the term *lower class* is heavily discouraged in American idiom and is being replaced by the SOCIAL WELFARE LINGO word *disadvantaged.*)

In the democratic world of free enterprise, supposedly bereft of privilege, there can be no *first class,* or, at least, that is what the abolishers of *first class* want people to believe. Reducing the ability of idiomatic American English to differentiate classes of wealth and power is reminiscent of the semantic gymnastics performed in old Soviet Russia and modern communist China.

First class does still exist on long-distance passenger trains and cruise ships, two systems of transportation from past decades. The sound of *first class* is apparently acceptable only when it echoes within acknowledged cultural relics.

Flaccid phrasing is created when a present participle is padded with an auxiliary verb such as *am, are,* or *is.* Explaining this clumsy construction takes more time than it does to fix it.

I am hoping that things work out.
[I hope that things work out.]

We want to know what you are thinking.
[We want to know what you think.]

Focus on is by far the most capacious STUFFING phrase in modern American idiom. It has been substituting, incorrectly, for many words and phrases.

discuss (*Let's focus on that issue.*)
keep in mind (*The latter figure is the one the administration wants us to focus on.*)
satisfy (*The company has got to keep its eye on the ball and focus on its customers.*)
encourage (*The Nature Conservancy focuses on environmental preservation and conservation.*)
consider (*Substantial numbers of consumers fail to focus on the economics of their lease deal.*)
think about (*The sales rep will want you to focus on just one number—the monthly payment.*)
appeal to (*Advertisers were kind of slow to really focus on women.*)

Focus on and *focused on* have been so overworked that two substitutes, *concentrate on* and *oriented toward*, have been pressed into service to help out. Neither is an improvement.

The computer game maker is expected to concentrate on developing [develop] software for its former rivals.

American physicians are not oriented toward disease prevention. [American physicians are inclined to treat disease rather than prevent it.]

Formulate. To *formulate* something is to prepare it according to a formula. Baby food is formulated, so is nitroglycerin and the plot of a romance novel. Many, however, use the word as a showy substitute for *devise* or *prepare*, even if that preparation has no formula.

Formulate is also used in THE ROUNDABOUT WAY phrase *formulate a response*, as in *Jacobs asked for time to formulate a response*. The word *respond* would do just fine.

Free. *Give your parents six months of free e-mail and internet access*, reads an advertisement for a product that will track and record your parents' every move and then sell this information to other companies. *Sign up today for cool free stuff*, urges the banner heading a soft-drink company's Web page for young people, but *free* has a price: the address, age, sex, phone number, and a checklist of spending habits and entertainment preferences of the respondent.

A word of many meanings, *free* in such contexts means one thing only: "without charge." But the lack of an explicit fee does not mean that no cost is attached; a person's personal information and privacy have value, which is why companies are willing to barter for them.

Here are other dictionary definitions of *free* that do not apply to solicitations tied to the Internet:

not subject to the control or domination of another

not united with, attached to, or combined with something
else

not determined by anything beyond its own nature or
being

exempt, relieved, or released esp. from burdensome, noxious, or
deplorable condition or obligation

The use of *free* in phrases such as *free customer service* may be simply unnecessary, or it may be laying the groundwork for a future in which things that one naturally assumes would be free of charge—such as customer service—no longer will be.

Free-for-all verbs are principally the creations of advertising copywriters, but they also appear in academia, business, popular journalism, and everyday conversation. While there is no law against inventing one's own verbs, sometimes things get a little out of hand.

Please wait while your credit card is authorizing.

By linking it to tax benefits, we incent people to show commitment to parenting.

We're efforting to work this out.

She tried to guilt him into returning the money, but he refused.

The parents took it upon themselves to see to it that all the kids were journaling every day.

The smarter way to office!

Why must people conversate at the exit door?

See also -IZE VERBS, RE- VERBS, and JARGON GRIDLOCK.

Friendly. Only sentient beings can display friendship toward one another. The use of *friendly* as a sloppy synonym for *beneficial* leads to oddities such as *Len Hopper, ASLA president, believes that the interaction between buildings and the community should be friendly.*

Friendly also anchors some of the most loathsome HYPHEN-MONSTERS, e.g., *user-friendly, business-friendly, customer-friendly*.

Full Range. A *range* can be broad, wide, or long, as well as narrow or short. But to call a range *full*, as in *You'll enjoy a full range of exclusive cardmember benefits*, is to make a great show but say nothing.

Function has swallowed many concrete words, such as *task* or *job*.

These varied functions [tasks] still have to be performed with or without a truck.

Stress can affect your immune system, raise blood pressure, and skew hormonal function [activity].

Flashlight has beam and lantern functions. [The flashlight also serves as a lantern.]

Function is also used as a SECRET SNOB WORD to distinguish between a social gathering where money or status is paramount (black-tie function, business function, city hall function) and one in which the goal is mere sociability (birthday party, bachelor party, toga party).

Generate. When compared to ordinary words like *produce* and *create*, *generate* sounds impressive. Electricity and power are things that are generated. It is not surprising that a journalist seeking to enliven an article would borrow the word to say that *a new film generated excitement* or that *an appeals court ruling generated controversy.* Memo writers, seeing *generate* in this expanded role and unwisely trusting the lexical accuracy of the press, have begun to use it as well. *Generate* now describes the creation of reports and the production of trash, or anything else for which *produce* and *create* are no longer thought sufficiently thrilling.

> The plastic shortage has generated a recycling alliance.

> Our e-mail generates quality leads.

> The division generates too much paperwork.

Writers who have become dependent on *generate* are demanding more and more from it, transforming the word into a vehicle for STUFFING and leading to the following:

IMAX generates [earns] most of its cash by leasing sound and projection systems to theaters.

Overnight construction is generating [causing] traffic delays.

President Bush's tax proposals are generating [prompting] criticism from Democrats.

Some investigators have failed to appreciate these contradictions and have generated [reached] erroneous conclusions.

His ability to continually generate [attract] new fans has enabled him to headline Las Vegas resorts every year for 36 consecutive years.

If you're not using your computer to generate income [make money], you're leaving money on the table.

They hoped that hosting the Olympics would generate huge exposure and increased tourism [draw attention and boost tourism].

Go and **goes** are often used in place of *say* or *said* in recounting past conversation: *So he goes, What do you think? And I go, I don't know, what do you think?* It has become the established manner of reporting among those who have not been taught to avoid it, and most of us make this error at times even when we know better. The substitution of *say* for *go* in these sentences would not necessarily seem artificial to the people who use *go* habitually, but purposeless.

Grow. Financial journalists and copywriters have blurred the distinction between the metaphorical and the literal use of the verb *grow* by using it in phrases such as *grow your income* and *grow your investment*, a peculiar approach to expressing the idea of *making money*, and the corruption has spread rapidly. *Grow* now operates as a clumsy synonym for *expand, increase,* and *broaden.*

> You need to grow your job search.

> How can we grow our membership?

> Philip Morris has grown its efforts to communicate more openly with the public.

> Earnings will be lower than expected because of the cost of growing our wireless business.

> The fundamental question is, do we grow the government or do we trust people to invest their own money?

Grow has also muscled aside another metaphor, *build.*

> All these mavericks with no credentials, high-school dropouts who couldn't get a loan, grew one of the nation's most powerful industries.

> I want to grow this relationship.

The last example, when used romantically, is an especially ugly way to say *I want us to spend more time together* or *I think I love you.*

Hassle-free carries a heavy implication of dissatisfaction. *Want a hassle-free way to shop for the things your children need?* implies that the way you shop now for the things your children need is full of unpleasantness, while *This is the way to do all your online banking hassle-free* implies that the way you're presently doing either on-line or real-world banking is a burdensome chore, and *Take advantage of this free, no-hassle service. It's painless and stress-free!* implies a familiarity with hassle, pain, and stress that is not reassuring.

The popularity of *hassle-free* as a sales tool is perhaps the result of our era of negative campaigning, when being the lesser of two evils constitutes a virtue. In contrast to CONVENIENCE, a word frequently used in similar contexts, *hassle-free* merely promises neutrality, not pleasure; it offers the reward of not being assaulted, of freedom from grief. It is an odd creation of a frustrating time.

Hey is gradually replacing *hi*—which itself replaced *hello*—as an introductory word of greeting, the trend in our society being toward ever greater informality. It is particularly jarring in written communication, where it is sometimes all that introduces a letter: *Hey* instead of *Hey, Ken* (or *hey ken;* see CAPITAL OFFENSES).

Holy War? The religious and the secular have each gained a surprising foothold in infiltrating today's lexicon, nudging aside words that may evoke the opposing point of view. We say that we will *evolve* a business or technology, displacing the old-fashioned words *develop* and *improve* (although any biologist will tell you that *evolution* does not mean improvement but change). Also on humanism's side is the wholesale replacement of *inspire* and *inspirational* by *motivate* and *motivational,* even in instances where the former clearly would be the better words: *Our goal is to motivate you to do what's best for yourself and those you care about.*

God, Allah, and Yahweh have Their victories as well. It's no longer fashionable to speak of the *origin* of an idea, but of its *genesis;* celebrities no longer give *endorsements,* but *testimonials;* the nation's drug policy may be beyond *salvation,* not *hope;* a secular program or cause is frequently a *crusade;* and the child or artist we once lauded as *smart* or *talented* is now *gifted.*

Hyphen-Monsters. It is easy—too easy—to invent new words by joining together other or parts of other words with hyphens rather than use existing words. EUPHEMISMS such as *pro-life* and *pro-choice* allow their users to avoid saying what would be politically disagreeable, while a hybrid like *age-defying* gives an advertiser a bold way to say that a product keeps you from looking as old as you are.

Not all hyphen-monsters are bad. Some reinforce the tone of what is being said or add a rhythm or spark that conveys meaning, as in *Wednesday's opening night hype-o-rama generated the usual buzz from the national media* or *The days right before your period are especially crave-crazy,* but most add nothing but feeble novelty, and the worst lack even that.

A tour through Old England makes an enchanting complement to this invaluable, life-benefiting program.

"It wasn't the suit on the brother but the brother in the suit that got you respect," says Freddie in one of the film's many faux-dramatic moments.

This needed reform should be accompanied by a strong maintenance-of-effort requirement to ensure that state aid increases actually go to classrooms.

The ancient art of placement can help one to either find that person with whom one can find at-one-ment or help us to create at-one-ment with the person we are currently with.

Hyphen-monsters occur frequently in SOCIAL WELFARE LINGO.

Impact connotes the striking of one thing against another, a collision, and by extension, its effect on the object struck. Used figuratively, as a cheap substitute for *affect* or EFFECT, it has become one of the most common words in junk English. A writer who has nothing more definitive to say than *Inflation has had an effect on income* will instead write *Inflation has had an impact on income;* a speaker who can make only the tepid observation that *The President can affect health care costs* can instead say *The President can impact health care costs;* and both can then pose as someone not afraid to forcefully state the facts.

In the examples that follow, *affect* or *effect* can be substituted for *impact*, but all this does is make clear that nothing is being said.

Make a well-informed decision which will impact your future today!

Should rolling blackouts occur, a lack of power to light homes and run computers may not be the only impact residents are likely to experience. Natural gas appliances impacted might include cooktops, ovens, clothes dryers, and forced-air furnaces. Most wall and floor furnaces and water heaters are not likely to be affected.

The vast majority of debate stories (74 percent) were written in a way that mostly impacted candidates and their campaigns. Interestingly, they were twice as likely to impact Gore's candidacy as they were to impact Bush's. Citizens were left out. Only 15 percent of the debate stories were written in ways that made clear the impact on citizens.

In this last example the writer wanted to make a point, but his or her reliance on *impact* instead of specifics made it unintelligible.

The popularity of *impact* has led to the coining of a gruesome adjective, *impactful*, as in *The company intends to make this marketing campaign highly impactful.*

In terms of and its cousins, *as reflected by* and *is relative to*, are surplus phrases that are used more in speech than in writing. While in speech one may rush to key points before thinking through how to connect the parts of a sentence, when writing one should not—as is clear from the following examples.

This is the largest oil spill, in terms of volume, in the history of offshore drilling.

Iowa's economy remains strong, as reflected by its low jobless rate.

Indicate. To *indicate* is to give a signal, to point out. To use the word as a synonym for *say*—as if there aren't already enough sloppy synonyms for that word—is technically correct, but it reduces the worth of a verb that would otherwise convey a useful shade of meaning.

> He has indicated that he has seen the light and is desirous of turning his life around.
>
> Moore indicated that the most vulnerable properties would be older buildings in fringe locations.

Indicate has fallen victim to its own popularity and is now one of the most popular STUFFING words, employed for an ever-widening range of meaning.

> The chart indicated [illustrated] a sharp downturn in sales in the third quarter.
>
> All valet parking lots are clearly indicated [marked].
>
> Long's report did not indicate [reveal] if Satterfield had used the NCIC system.
>
> Please indicate [note] if you have more than one appliance.
>
> There are growing indications [signs] that Dreifort is set to re-sign with Los Angeles. And there have been indications [rumors] he could wind up with a deal similar to the one Kevin Brown received two years ago.

Individualize and **personalize** are narrower than their cousins *customize* and *optimize;* it is tailoring done for an audience of one. They have come to overshadow other words such as *individual* and *personal*, as well as *private, specific, custom, select, exclusive*, and UNIQUE.

A personalized [unique] number will be assigned to you, which you should write in the boxes on your enrollment form.

To make the ring truly unique, it will be individually personalized [engraved] for each alumnus.

Remember your favorite store, where personalized [personal] service was why you returned?

For individualized [individual] assistance, call us at our 24-hour help line.

Initiate is a favorite of those who believe that polysyllabic words elevate mundane writing. It started appearing as a synonym for *begin—We recently initiated [began] budget development for the third quarter*—but it apparently sounds so impressive to some that it now serves as a blanket substitute.

The Alliance says it already has initiated [filed] a half-dozen lawsuits against factory farm operations.

The whole world is waiting to see what changes Fox will initiate [make].

For the past two years the company has initiated [hosted] focus groups to determine what it is consumers want.

In a similar spirit, *initiative* has become popular with politicians and those who write about them as a dynamic substitute for the passive bureaucratic *plan* or *program*. This may make sense polit-ically, but it is nonsense English, and it has turned *initiative* into just another CHEAPENED WORD.

> The President's health care initiative would cut welfare roles by an estimated 25 percent.

> Ferguson spearheaded the education initiative.

> Many are skeptical that Bush's budget initiative would produce results if adopted by Congress.

> Some fear that the President's call for "a new public safety initiative" will result in even stricter parole supervision.

> "More job related programs, educational programs, and access to low income housing are what we need, but this initiative won't make a dent in those issues," he says.

Invisible Diminishers. *Perfect* and *foolproof* are words that every advertising and public-relations writer would love to use but cannot, as they demand standards that are rarely met. Thus invisible diminishers are called into service, words and phrases used to inconspicuously reduce the promise of powerful words. A cleaning product leaves glasses *virtually* spotless; an erroneous statement from a powerful person is *basically* or *essentially* or *fundamentally* or *substantially* true; a drug will *help* prevent hair loss; a diamond is *nearly* flawless, a brassiere *practically* weightless, a leather sofa on sale for *as much as* 50% off and *as little as* $39.95 a month. The trick relies on the human tendency to skip ahead while reading and the spokesperson's ability to downplay the diminisher and emphasize the words that follow. The sham is usually fleeting; once the seller has attracted the potential buyer's attention SELF-DECEPTION and the seller's persuasive skills will close the deal.

The success of invisible diminishers has led to the emergence of invisible inflators.

> Please allow 30 minutes or more for delivery.

> This product has been shown to be completely without significant side effects.

Issue. The current fashion of calling every problem an *issue* comes from SELF-HELP JARGON, where referring to one's problems as *issues* sounds less judgmental. There are no longer *problems* to *solve* but *issues* to *resolve* (or *address*), and while some favor the word on the merits of tact or politeness, its modern overuse smacks more of circumvention than courtesy.

> Many adults choose to smoke, notwithstanding the serious health issues surrounding smoking.

> He is a guy that is trying to work through some issues.

> Splitting the country would not solve the issue of the Florida election.

> She has weight issues.

> We have discipline issues at this school.

"If the states who participate in the program use the money to pick up more parole violators," she said, "I think there will be issues."

It was our understanding that any medical issues were resolved.

The issue has been researched, escalated, and is currently undergoing evaluation.

In the last example, from a form letter reply to a customer complaint, not only has *problem* been turned into *issue*, but the personal pronoun *Your* has been bumped by an impersonal *The*. Lexically, your problem has already ceased to exist.

-Ize Verbs. Adding *-ize* to a noun changes it to a verb. To *popularize* something means to cause something to become popular. The ways in which this simple Greek suffix can be used has broadened over time; for example, it can now mean to form something into the noun (*unionize*), treat it like the noun (*idolize*), engage in activity described by the noun (*philosophize*), become something metaphorically like the noun (*humanize*), and so on.

There are no rules to prevent the endless creation of *-ize* verbs; we often see *democratize* for *make fair*, *marginalize* for *belittle*, *prioritize* for *decide what's most important*, and *monetize* and *normalize*, whose meanings escape definition, hence their popularity with financial analysts and politicians. *Smartize*, the worst yet, was coined by a consultant who wanted to call attention to his employee education program.

Galvanize, *materialize*, and *realize* are fine words when used correctly, but they are often used as unnatural substitutes for *excite*, *happen*, and *reach* because some believe they make what they have to say sound more impressive. We say *conceptualize, finalize, utilize*, and *incentivize* because verbs like *imagine, complete, use*, and *encourage* seem too common.

The prefix *re-* is sometimes added to *-ize* verbs as an intensifier; hence monstrosities such as *reenergize, revitalize*, and *reconceptualize*.

The Bush administration will try to reenergize the sanctions imposed after Iraq's 1990 invasion of Kuwait.

The relationship between ethics and environment has to be reconceptualized as an interactive rather than a one-way affair.

Jargon Gridlock. To dismiss a jargon outright is to overlook its usefulness within its community. The hip-hop performer who tells an interviewer, *I'm not going for the chickenhead audience, I'm going for the macks and the players*, or the hacker who writes on an Internet message board, *Dike out that goto or the code police will get you*, are unintelligible to most of the world, but they are perfectly clear to their audiences.

Problems arise when jargon users forget that others do not share their specialized vocabulary—like when a social scientist tells a newspaper journalist, *Systems for structuring meaning through digitization of knowledge underlie a specific geocultural model; the risk is that it may impose as a criterion of universality a particular mode of thinking and feeling*.

Wall Street English is notorious for gridlocking understanding, even in a society where stock trading is no longer an exclusive activity of the wealthy but a form of mass recreation. It is particularly perplexing when applied to nonfinancial topics, such as in this quote from an article found in the sports section of a tabloid newspaper about the signing of Alex Rodriguez, a baseball player, to a multimillion-dollar contract: *This amount of money spread out over ten years could probably buy three franchises or so at the bottom end of market value. It's incredible. It's a straight upward trend that doesn't look like it will augur at all.*

The marketing analyst would understand the following entry in a brief dictionary of terms written by "the world's most accomplished and internationally recognized branding and design consultancy," but the ordinary reader—the intended audience—would not.

Descriptor: A term used with a brand name to communicate an informational attribute (e.g., variant, function, occasion, or target segment) about a specific offer.

This is pure junk English, but it is also a jargon. To those outside the reach of the vernacular, both the term being defined and its definition are meaningless.

Our language is awash in jargons. Plain English, unaffected idiom, and basic vernacular are gradually disappearing. Our preference for the specialized words we use to communicate within our own narrow groups is making us less able to communicate with everyone else.

Just. The word *just* is intended to serve as camouflage when attached to a command, blanketing the task demanded with the notion that it is simple and easy to perform:

Just rewrite that opening scene.

You just have to move that one pipe a few inches.

Usually *just* unintentionally conveys either the arrogance or the ignorance of the person issuing the command, or both, since that person obviously has no idea of the difficulty of the task.

Just is frequently enlisted by advertising copywriters to imply that an activity, price, or a period of time is astonishingly effortless or generous, or that an existing thing is trivial compared to what is being sold.

Just $59.95!

For starters, our value club is more than just a checking account.

You'll save money with just one low payment.

Your balance will be just $19.95 a month.

To consolidate your bills, just write a check.

The area has much more to offer the visitor than just world class Steelhead, Salmon, and Halibut fishing.

Lack of will describes the five words—*can, could, may, might, should*—that are used in advertising to avoid *will*. *Will* promises a result—in the following examples, the result the reader wants—but lack-of-will words do not.

The addition of the phrase *but probably will not* to the end of each of these sentences would give a more accurate sense of what is actually being said.

Bad credit? Too many debts? Bankruptcy may solve your problem!

By using our product you can save literally hundreds of dollars.

If you have a faulty joint or hip replacement you may qualify for a big cash settlement.

You might save enough this winter to pay for a vacation next summer!

This product can stimulate the COMPLETE re-growth of lost hair in as little as six months!

Level. Political leaders and advertisers pledge that what they are selling will take us to the *next level*, or *new levels*, or a *higher level*. City residents complain of the *noise level*, *entry-level* workers seek a *comfort level* in their jobs and hope someday to make it to *management level*, or maybe even the *executive level*. Abusing *level* this way, as an anchor for vague concepts and FAT-ASS PHRASES, telegraphs that what has been said will have to be decoded.

> Whatever your product, service or idea we can help take you to new levels [you sell more of it].

> If you've helped with a contribution in the past, please do your best to help again at the same level [match it]. If you're able to help at a higher level [give even more] this year, your donation will further help us reach our goal.

> Move your personal production or your business sales to the next level. [Sell more.]

Lifestyle. The meaning of the word *lifestyle* is a mystery. Sometimes it is used as a sloppy synonym for *life*, as in *Do you dream of a better lifestyle for yourself and your family?* At other times it apparently defines something, although that something is never clear. *Ashford offers sunglasses, fragrances, pens, men's and women's accessories, and home and lifestyle gifts* at least tells us some of the things that *lifestyle* is not. The word is widely used by home-furnishing and personal-hygiene retailers, credit-card companies, and illustrated-book publishers, who count on the general public recognizing what it stands for, if not exactly what it is.

Limited is a word often used by advertisers to impart an appearance of scarcity. *These funds are limited. Supplies are limited. Don't miss this limited time opportunity. Only a limited number will be made available.* Limited to how many, or to how much time? A million? Twenty years?

The continued abuse of *limited* is coming back to haunt those who practice it, as seen in this warning that appeared in a credit card solicitation: *No preset spending limit does not mean unlimited spending.*

Machine Language. Some people have had their English so debased—possibly it was never based to begin with—that they write and talk as if they were robots. Sometimes machine language is deliberate, an effort to lull the reader into oversight. In most cases, however, it appears that those who produce this mechanical, numbing monotone simply know no better and believe that they are communicating their ideas and feelings to the rest of the English-speaking world.

Sentences such as *Specific partnership objectives include promoting sustainable development in designs and project administration* and *Declination of any one study does not impact the solicitation of member support for future research efforts* deaden rather than awaken interest, as if they had been assembled from a series of binary equations.

The information you provide to our database of financial experts will result in offer's meeting the criterion you requested.

Consumption of chocolate is positively correlated with total dietary intake of copper.

We maximized the U.S. role but our results were minimal. We have over-used presidential impact. There may be value in letting the parties engage by themselves on a situational level.

The museum must foster an appreciation of those who strived to create societal environments conducive to human growth and development.

Anxiety presents itself as the overwhelming worry of a generalized anxiety disorder.

The emphasis was on alternatives coming from the countries experiencing most acutely the negative effects of globalization.

With this clarification, the independent functional principle adds overriding performance constraints to the structural design, based on system engineering concepts.

Without objective baseline indicators, it will not be possible to determine whether the stated goal of a net positive environmental impact for the Winter Games has been achieved.

This is an all-natural solution that neutralizes with pharmaceutical potency the low-grade inflammatory process associated with genetic hair loss.

With this important knowledge, ingenuity, and available equipment, the most effective way to optimize your operations will be a benefit to every operation.

We will facilitate a panel discussion with principals instrumental in the reconstitution of the service delivery system that highlight the training and operational dynamics of the "work-in-progress."

The participant will be provided legal tips for recognizing the potential liability incident and effective documentation techniques to minimize future legal impacts.

Major, Massive, Serious, Significant. *Major* changes, *massive* layoffs, *serious* money, *significant* damage —it is the current fashion to hurl about *major, massive, serious,* and *significant*—and *real,* on occasion—as if they were interchangeable and as if they were perfect synonyms for *comprehensive, considerable, extraordinary, huge, important, large, lavish, overwhelming, powerful, severe, substantial, sweeping, vast,* and *vigorous.*

Something that is *major*—of these four words, the one whose meaning most nearly approximates its popular usage—is not merely important or big, it is more than ordinarily important, or greater. *Hong Kong is a major world port. The major part of Michelangelo's work was of biblical subjects.*

Massive denotes mass and should strictly apply only to things that have large amounts of it: foundations, asteroids, pyramids, and the like. It has a history of metaphorical employment, but its expressiveness has been worn away by overuse.

Serious connotes something that is thoughtful, sober, or earnest: *a serious person; taking a serious look at one's life; only serious inquiries need apply.*

Significant carries connotations of consequence and expressiveness: *a significant glance; the significant details in a political settlement.*

To resort to these words again and again does not cause misunderstanding—everyone knows what is meant by *a major traffic jam, massive amounts of paperwork, serious earnings potential,* or *significant savings*—but it robs them of their specificity. Not too many years ago if one read that the New York City blizzard of 1888 was *a significant snowstorm*, one understood that it had significance; not just that it was big. A *real* problem was one that was not imaginary, not one that was just difficult.

Marketing. *Your marketing campaign will speed with pinpoint accuracy to your desired audience! Marketing* is used as a EUPHEMISM for *selling* or *sales*, and occasionally as a synonym for *promoting* when the word *selling* would give the wrong connotation, e.g., *marketing your business*.

The word *marketing* was probably coined to make people feel better about working in sales, or to make potential customers forget they were being talked to by salespeople.

Mirage words are used by advertising copywriters in place of words we want to see, chosen in the hope that they will present the image of those words while expressing a meaning that is something less. Thus one encounters the phrases *doctor-recommended* instead of *-approved*, *cold remedy* for *cold cure*, *water-repellent* or *rust-resistant* for *-proof*, and *scientifically validated* for *proven*. Mirage words rely on SELF-DECEPTION.

Mode. Aside from its use in the term *fashion mode*, where it is synonymous with *style*, *mode* most frequently appears idiomatically as an unnecessary appendage. A person in a *thinking mode* is thinking, a *writing mode* writing, a *working mode* working. Adding *mode* to such unremarkable activities makes them sound more machinelike and thus smart to some.

Moderate. *With a moderate population, Florham Park is a congenial, suburban-residential community, with some light industry.* The citizens of Florham Park know firsthand the difficulty of working with a language that lacks a good adjective to fit between *large* and *small*. A *medium* population would not sound right, a *fair* or *modest* or *nominal* population would sound tepid, and an *average* population would sound more like a sneer at the character of Florham Park's residents than a description of their number. *Fair-* or *medium-sized* would at least not leave the reader wondering what the population is moderate in.

The use of *moderate* in the term *moderate people skills* is a mutilation of the already monstrous.

Negative. People have developed an aversion to saying anything bad (see also ISSUE and SPEAK NO EVIL), so it is not surprising that a word has come to serve to keep us from saying even the word *bad* itself. That word is *negative*.

> She clammed up and refused to say anything negative [bad] about her husband or her marriage.

> Zero tolerance in school may sound like a good idea in theory, but it sends a negative [bad] message to the children who are punished by the system.

More precise and powerful words could have replaced *negative* in the above examples—*disagreeable, nasty, sickening, awful, offensive*—but *bad*, although inexact, is at least better than the timid *negative*. The weakness of the word encourages flaccid construction around it. Even writers who want to make a strong statement fall victim, turning what should have been forceful into something feeble:

The Sopranos rates with *Birth of a Nation* and the *Protocols of the Elders of Zion* in inculcating a compelling negative image of [vilifying, libeling, defaming, demeaning, etc.] a people.

The popularity of *negative* among those who never want to say anything unpleasant has led to its being incorporated into phrases that extend its reach. *Negative feedback* is now the way to say *unfavorable reaction* or *criticism*, and *negative aspects, negative effects,* and *negatives* have replaced words such as *hazards, drawbacks, risks,* and *dangers.*

The negative aspects of irradiating the nation's meat supply far outweigh the positives.

Negative has also replaced the words *critical* and *pessimistic*—two words we also apparently no longer wish to say; the latter is itself a replacement for *glum*—in the idiomatic expression *Don't be so negative.*

Nonprofit. A common confusion is that a *nonprofit* or *not-for-profit* organization is one that exists for the general welfare rather than for private gain. After all, if an organization doesn't exist to make a profit, its purpose—and, by proxy, the intent of the people who work within it—must be noble and altruistic.

Nonprofit or *not-for-profit,* however, apply only to the accounting methods used by the organization and have no bearing on what positions the organization supports. And while the organization cannot by law make a profit, the individuals within it can. Many nonprofit executives profit handsomely from their work.

To be sure, the work done by many nonprofits is worthy, but some are formed by PR firms to further the interests of their corporate clients and are given impartial-sounding names. The nonprofit Credit Research Center, for example, furthers the interests of credit card companies, and the nonprofit Consumer Alert is funded by big business to muddle the charges leveled against bad products by the independent Consumers Union.

Obese prepositions are used in place of simple conjunctions and prepositions, or comparatively simple compound prepositions. They are often heard in speech, particularly on news shows where spokespeople utter them as they think of something meaningful to say. This is understandable, if awkward, circumlocution, but these constructions should never appear in print. Following are some representative examples.

as far as the _____ is concerned	as for the _____
due to the fact that	since
for the purpose of	to
in as much as because of	since
in order to	to
in the area of	around
in the instance of	as for
in the matter of	about
in the neighborhood of	around
in the region of	near
in view of the fact that	since
is much the same as	is like
is relative to	is like

of the character of	like
of the nature of	like
on account of	because of
on the order of	about
owing to the fact that	because of
relating to the subject matter of	regarding
so as to	to
the purpose of which is	to
with regards to the creation of	as for

100%. Americans, a practical people, have always been a little uneasy with concepts that cannot be expressed in numbers—love, death, beauty, etc.—which perhaps explains why advertisers use the mathematical expression *100%* so frequently. The fraction is almost always unnecessary, and no meaning would be lost if it was removed from assertions such as *Our service is 100% free; This plan is 100% ethical; Money back if you are not 100% completely satisfied; We 100% guarantee this product is for you; All information will remain 100% confidential;* and the pithy *100% real*. We obviously find its presence reassuring.

The allure of *100%*, however, has been cheapened by the same spokespeople and copywriters who originally made it desirable. A day's reading will turn up at least one sentence such as *Our employees give 200%* or *If the competition gives 100% we must give 110%*. Resorting to a mathematically impossible fraction to express ourselves shows how the prevalence of hype has reduced some to uttering nonsense.

See also PARASITIC INTENSIFIERS.

Opportunity. A radio commercial selling an airline's newly added routes speaks not of *options*, nor even of *possibilities*, but of expanded travel *opportunities*, as if each ticket promised success, not just another seat. *Take this opportunity to tell us your income objectives* is the copywriter's way of dressing up *Fill out our questionnaire. Is there any question that this is an incredible opportunity?* glorifies a junk-mail offer for a cell phone. And *An opportunity like this only comes around once a year!* is a recasting of a President's Day sale.

True opportunities are rarely advertised.

Overworked Emphasizers. The need to outshout those shouting around us has resulted in many overworked adjectives, adverbs, and a few verbs as well. Some are badly mishandled, as when *tremendous* is used in place of *large*. *He was offered a tremendous amount of money. Crucial* is frequently employed to describe what may be *decisive* or merely *important*.

Emphasizers have become imperfect replacements for concise if humble words such as *interesting, large, many*, and *very*. The most overworked emphasizers, such as *remarkable*, are substitutes for all:

> a remarkable [interesting] story you won't want to miss
>
> the number of responses was remarkable [large]
>
> a remarkable amount of [many] people
>
> this mattress is remarkably [very] soft

Emphasizers make for an artificially emphatic world in which, paradoxically, nothing stands out. The danger of all this cacophony is that we may eventually grow accustomed to it and then expect emphasizers in everything. Our careers, relationships, appliances must thereafter be *awesome, incredible,* or at least *optimal,* or we will view our lives with dissatisfaction.

The following list is far from exhaustive.

bad
unconscionable

change
revolutionize

good
an absolute must (have), amazing, astounding, awesome, a classic, extraordinary, fabulous, fantastic, great, incredible, optimal, outstanding, remarkable, sensational, spectacular, superior, tremendous, ultimate, unbelievable, world class

important
alarming, core, critical, critically important, crucial, essential, integral, key, major, mission critical, quintessential, radical, remarkable, revolutionary, significant, spectacular, vital, vitally important, watershed

interesting
amazing, dynamic, incredible, intriguing, remarkable, spectacular, unbelievable

large
amazing, astronomical, awesome, considerable, enormous, gigantic, incalculable, incredible, major, mammoth, massive, outrageous, remarkable, spectacular, staggering, stupendous, substantial, tremendous, unbelievable, unfathomable, vast

many
an amazing number of, an astonishing number of,
an astronomical number of, an awesome number of,
a considerable number of, an enormous number of, a fantastic
number of, an incalculable number of, an incredible number
of, innumerable, a massive number of, an outrageous number
of, a remarkable number of, a shocking number of,
a significant number of, a spectacular number of, a staggering
number of, a stupendous number of, a substantial number of,
a tremendous number of, an unbelievable number of, an
unfathomable number of, a vast number of

much
an abundance of, an amazing amount of, an astonishing
amount of, an astronomical amount of, an awesome amount of,
a considerable amount of, an enormous amount of, a fantastic
amount of, an incalculable amount of, an incredible amount of,
an inordinate amount of, a massive amount of, an outrageous
amount of, a remarkable amount of, a shocking amount of,
a significant amount of, a spectacular amount of, a staggering
amount of, a stupendous amount of, a substantial amount of,
a tremendous amount of, an unbelievable amount of,
an unfathomable amount of, a vast amount of

new
revolutionary

special
exclusive

surprised
amazed, astounded, shocked

very
    alarmingly, amazingly, extremely, fabulously, highly,
incredibly, quintessentially, radically, remarkably, unbelievably,
vastly

well-liked
    acclaimed

Padding. Sometimes it seems that saying something simply is simply not enough. So we drop words into sentences to mildly emphasize nouns and verbs that either cannot be emphasized further or cannot be emphasized, period.

Popular padding words include *actual(ly)*, *basically*, *certainly*, *completely*, *definitely*, *essentially*, *indeed*, *literally*, *pure*, *surely*, *totally*, *veritable*, and *very*. A few examples will show them at work:

It might have been informative if some actual executives, whose jobs it is to actually do business in this supposedly out-of-control system, were invited to speak.

Sometimes there are more important things than just pure dollars.

What's basically happened is that the electricity providers are waiting until the last minute to put in bids for selling their power.

Order within the next 48 hours and receive free an amazing tool that will totally protect your computer from online break-in.

By using our refill system you can save literally hundreds of dollars.

I definitely concur.

For more vigorous padding, see PARASITIC INTENSIFIERS.

Palsy-Walsy Pitches. Few things are as irritating as a sales pitch cloaked in a lexical mantle of friendship. Its intent is to persuade you that this is not another intrusive attempt to separate you from your money but important or happy news being delivered from one friend to another, from the corporation to you. Such casual, intimate language is aimed not only at the potential customer; it is devised to brainwash the salesperson as well.

Here are some of the more common techniques of palsy-walsy pitches.

- Replacement of the terms *it* and *the company* with *we* and *us*, as if the solicitation comes from a family or a group of friendly people, not a business whose intention could not possibly be friendship:

  All we ask before we ship you your free pager is for you to allow us to provide the airtime for you.

  Funding borrowers with less than perfect credit is our specialty!

  We prepare everything with the same care and attention you would in your own kitchen.

  From our family to yours.

- Use of a deferential, even obsequious tone, characterizing the sales prospect as a partner or a superior:

> Thank you for being a cardmember.

> Allow us the opportunity to earn your business.

> We value the relationship we have built with you and your continued business is important to us.

> We're excited to offer you this 35mm camera as a special thank-you gift. It's your reward for being a valued customer.

> Please let us know if there is anything we can do to service your account.

- Use of bouncy, conversational English:

> Say good-bye to those holiday bills!

> Check out our web site!

> Guess what? We've got good news for you!

> E-Z benefits add up!

> Hey, we're talking 150 hours of internet service for only $15.00 a month!

- A transformation of the sales transaction into "helping" the sales prospect:

> Even if you're currently working with another lender or have been turned down before, we can still help.

These are just a few of the ways we can help.

Regardless of whether you have good or bad credit, we can help you.

- A recasting of unasked-for solicitations as wonderful prizes or honors to be received:

This exclusive offer provides members with special privileges not available to other cardholders.

You receive an instant 30% cashback bonus award at any of our participating dealers.

Partner in our AdvantagePlus Program and receive 5,000 bonus miles.

No other card offers the benefits of the Gold Advantage World MasterCard, in addition to the exclusive prizes that come with this offer.

People may be smart enough to know a palsy-walsy pitch when they see one. But the proliferation of this kind of sales talk is deliberately erasing a dividing line, turning friendship into something that can be bought.

Parasitic Intensifiers. Our age of hyperbole has bred a generation of writers who feel uneasy when a word is left to pull its own weight. It is not enough that a stock promises *growth*, it must promise *substantial* growth. It is not enough that a snack be *nutritious*, it must be *highly* nutritious. A gift is nothing unless it is *outright*, profit unexciting unless it is *pure*, a refund suspect unless it is *full*.

The danger here is that formerly strong words are being reduced to lightweights that need to be bulked up with intensifiers to regain their punch. To *offer insight* or to *oppose a position* now sound tepid unless the insight is *valuable* and the opposition *diametrical*. The intensifier drains the vigor from its host.

To use any intensifier is to signal that its accompanying word is weak for the job asked of it, or, more troubling, that it has been wasted through years of parasitic leeching. Those who no longer recognize enfeebled terms such as *total freedom* and *absolutely true* and *most unique* for what they are have stripped *freedom* and *true* and UNIQUE of their power.

Parasitic intensifiers number into the hundreds if not thousands.

(absolutely) essential, free, legal, nothing, perfect, true (*You'll get six steak burgers absolutely free!*)

(actual) earnings, results

(added) flexibility

(all the more) unique

(broad) generalization

(complete) details, shutdown

(completely) fixed, off, positive, satisfied, transformed (*This feature allows your pager to retrieve messages sent when your pager was out of range or turned completely off.*)

(coveted) honor

(critically) important

(dead) serious

(deeply) appreciative, divided

(definite) decision, plans

(definitely) true

(definitive) agreement (*Northwest and Continental boards approved the definitive agreement, which must still be approved by their stockholders.*)

(diametrically) opposed

(distinctly) true

(drastically) cut, reduced

(earnest) consideration

(effective) means

(entire) society (*Your contribution will help ensure a brighter future for our community and our entire society.*)

(enormously) popular

(exactly) preserve (*This technique exactly preserves the natural spectrum of vitamins, minerals, and protein.*)

(exceedingly) well

(exhaustive) research

(extremely) careful, grateful

(finally) accepted, convinced, decided

(formally) accepted, convinced, decided

(full) refund, shutdown

(fully) approve, endorse, evaluate, guarantee, investigate (*Bally has fully investigated these complaints and believes they are completely without merit.*)

(further) insures, proves

(genuine) superstar

(grand) opening

(great) opportunity, pride

(heartfelt) thanks

(highly) accurate, complex, dynamic, impressed, nutritious, profitable, qualified, recommended, volatile (important) opportunity

(incredible) hardships

(incredibly) accurate, expensive

(integral) part

(jam) packed

(literally) true

(more) literate, seriously (*Please remember that your comments are taken more seriously if you maintain a polite tone.*)

(most) unique, welcome (*We deliver the most unique direct e-mail marketing campaign in the world.*)

(ongoing) commitment

(outright) gift, lie

(phenomenal) growth

(pinpoint) accuracy

(precision) engineered

(proper) care

(pure) profit

(quite) amused, amusing, fascinated, fascinating, good, interested, interesting, intrigued, intriguing, possible, possibly, similar, welcome

(radical) change

(rank) amateur

(real) danger, facts, profit, test (*Many have been conditioned to believe it must be illegal, immoral, or unethical to ever earn any real profits from our efforts.*)

(relatively) few

(right) now

(serious) consideration, crisis, desire, thought (*There is no experience necessary. However you must have a serious desire for a personal and financial change.*)

(solid) data

(specific) categories, details, information, reasons

(substantial) growth, potential

(total) cost, freedom, impact, price (*Many people in our enterprise retire wealthy in 2 to 3 years and have total freedom.*)

(totally) complete, ignored, reputable, satisfied, transformed

(true) facts, professional

(truly) free, impressive, meet, transformed, unfortunate, unique

(ultimate) goal, resolution

(undue) alarm, concern

(unexpected) surprise

(uniquely) qualified

(valuable) insight, opportunity

(vast) majority

(very) big, careful, complex, important, impressive, substantial, thankful, unique, urgent

(vitally) important

(well) aware, satisfied

The Passive Voice. In the English language there are only two voices—passive and active. The active voice is what most people use in everyday writing and conversation: *We went to the movies; I like pizza; Everyone knows that politicians are crooks.* The passive voice, much maligned, is appropriate when the identity of a person stating a fact is less important than the fact itself. *It was decided that the tomb should remain sealed to avoid contamination.* Scholarly texts are often written in the passive voice; in places this book is, too. The passive voice is also appropriate as a way to add emphasis to certain words in a sentence by moving them to the end.

One vote confirmed the ruling, although active, is not as strong as the passive *The ruling was confirmed by one vote*.

The passive voice is widely used in politics and corporate PR as a way to evade responsibility. A letter from a government representative's office reads *Mistakes were made* rather than *I made mistakes;* a spokesperson for a corporation says *The river was found to be polluted at the plant site* rather than *Our plant polluted the river*. By eliminating personal pronouns (*I, we*) and changing the subject of the sentence from a thing acting to a thing being acted upon, persons or organizations who might be held accountable are pushed into the background or removed altogether.

Those who employ the passive voice often combine it with flat phrasing and confusing circumlocution to bury the truth.

Since inclusion can be considered recognition of career position and professionalism, each candidate has been evaluated in keeping with optimal standards of individual achievement.

[Our organization admits only the best people.]

With the availability of an internet enrollment process, the need for clerical staff has been reduced.

[The college will fire clerical workers now that enrollment is on-line.]

These price changes were made necessary due to substantial increases in the market price of natural gas being experienced nationwide.

[The company has to pay more for natural gas, so now you will, too.]

People Reduction. The words *people* and *person* are rapidly disappearing from our lexicon, often replaced by *individuals* and *individual,* examples of ARTIFICIAL VOCABULARY. What's more, the world of commerce has busily been inventing many new, cold synonyms for *you* and *I: the client base, the consumer base, the consumer market, target market, target segment, demographic, resources, end users.* To see a *person* as a *consumer*—what used to be called a *customer* (a word that lives on mainly in the term *valued customer*)—is natural to those who sell, although the absence of *people* in their vocabulary uncomfortably parallels the way language is used to divest soldiers of human qualities.

The nearly inescapable *consumers* has become a cold synonym for many more accurate and human terms. We are gradually being turned into creatures whose only defining characteristic is that we shop:

> Consumers should check their medicine cabinet once a year for medications that are expired or are no longer being used.

> Firestone issued a statement denying that the tires were a hazard to consumers.

> The average consumer uses nearly 13 pounds of PET plastic each year, according to the National Association for PET Container Resources.

Positive, the most popular of all SELF-HELP JARGON words, is often used redundantly.

> Hampton gave the new ballpark a positive endorsement.

Learn what positive steps you can take to help.

People have found *positive* so appealing that they often attach it to other words to build gutless new phrases such as *positive aspects, positive attitude, positive feedback, positive outlook,* and *positive approach*. As with STUFFING words, *positive* has become something we use automatically, ousting *good, cheerful, confident, upbeat, favorable,* and *beneficial* from our lexicon, words that, although clearer, somehow seem not positive enough.

It's not my place to comment other than to say I feel confident the situation will be resolved quickly and positively.

The last two weeks have been positive for the Bush administration.

Let's try and be positive about this.

The Chinese ambassador gave a positive account of the talks.

The two organizations must work together to ensure the impact of federal buildings on their communities is positive.

Privatize, one of the most commonly heard of the new -IZE VERBS, can be translated into *run as a business to make money*. When we are sold the benefits of *privatizing* our schools, our prisons, our social welfare system, we are reminded of the words *private* or *privacy* or *private enterprise*, all of which sound like a good thing. We think of *efficiency* and *accountability*—the *run as a business* part of the definition, not the *to make money* part. Nevertheless, the need to make money more likely than not outweighs any efficiencies that might be introduced in the system, which often ends up in worse shape than before it became privatized. If we were told that our child's school was going to be *run as a business to make money*, we'd probably be inclined to challenge the ethicality of such an arrangement. But *privatize*, assertive and vaguely promising, raises no such misgivings.

Privatize often appears in tandem with a word similar in spirit, *deregulate*, and has a close relation in the clumsy HYPHEN-MONSTER *for-profit*, which is sometimes used by journalists and occasionally by businesspeople, but never by politicians, who know better. If *privatize* were merged with *for-profit* to create a more honest word, *profitize*, how willing would we be to turn over our social institutions to the eager new owners?

Proactive, the combination of a positive prefix, *pro-*, and a dynamic adjective, *active*, is popularly used to mean *taking charge of one's own destiny*, without having to specify how.

> "This administration is not standing still," a source said Tuesday. "They're being very proactive."

> Parents and schools are going to have to get a lot more proactive in providing information to balance the images of sex that young people get on the Net.

The success of *proactive* may encourage monster makers to introduce new freaks into our language, and it may not be long before we speak of things as *proinnovative*, *pronutritious*, or *proproductive*.

Process gets under the skin of those who become aware of its presence. The word is used to dress up plain English with an imagined air of sophistication and depth; *thinking* becomes *the thought process; getting old, the aging process; education, the learning process;* and so on and on and on.

The needlessness of *process* is evident by the ease with which it can be removed from many sentences in which it appears.

> Adversarialism characterized the whole election process.

> We think that this process is entirely unjustified.

> I'm sure there was just as much melon wasted in the carving process as was eaten by the guests.

Sometimes people replace *process* with other, equally gray nouns such as *treatment,* SYSTEM, or *procedure*—but habitual *process* users rarely achieve clarity through substitution.

> These monitoring procedures are key to the success of our system.

> Sometimes it may seem that the minority factor is overriding the treatment, but sometimes it's the situation.

Project. The same people who have long used *projected* as an unnecessary synonym for *estimated* now use *project* as an unnecessary synonym for *estimate. The administration projects the budget* *deficit this year at $4.5 billion.* The word *guess* would give the meaning most clearly, but those who make guesses never call them that, and in what is perhaps codependency at work, those whose livelihood is made from reporting guesses never translate the EUPHEMISM into plain English.

Quality, an empty noun, has been put to work as an empty adjective.

Would you like a quality relationship, but work so many hours you don't have time to look for that special person?

Proud manufacturers of leading cigarette brands such as Marlboro, Virginia Slims, Benson & Hedges, and other quality brands.

Quality service begins with quality employees.

Quality sounds better than *good* or *goodness* to many people, and they use it as a synonym.

We acknowledge the fact that he is a quality player that any and all teams would love to have.

The protestors loudly denounced the lack of quality programming.

Those of us who care about the quality of our society must take steps to assure that organizations like this one thrive.

The widespread abuse of *quality* has spawned an equally empty phrase, *quality of life*, which is employed by those who wish to sound authoritative and yet be spared the tiresome responsibility of details.

> We all want a better quality of life.
>
> Inconsiderate tenants have destroyed our quality of life.
>
> Higher quality products for a higher quality of life.

Quite is frequently used as an intensifier to impart an air of sophistication to writing or speech. But to say that one is *quite excited* is to add nothing to the concept, and to write that something is *quite amusing* or *quite interesting* is to knock the wind out of words that already lack vigor. *Very* is better; it clearly boosts the intensity of the word it is tacked to and avoids pretentiousness.

Writers should resist the temptation to replace *quite* with the even less forceful intensifiers *fairly* and *most*. They will only make matters worse.

> Animal escapes are fairly common at the zoo and are most exciting.

Quotation marks are not a substitute for italics. They can be used to call attention to unusual words or phrases that a writer either invented or felt needed emphasis in a particular sentence. This, however, sometimes carries with it the implication "so-called," or suggests that what is written is not what it appears to be. That was obviously not the intent in the following sentences.

Cooked to order; never "pre-cooked" like others.

Each year in the U.S. alone, the "postal" bulk mail industry consumes over 450 million trees just to make the paper used in sending their advertisements and promotions.

The oil companies can phase out fossil fuels and guarantee the strength of their company for the future, and at the same time make the "environmentalists" their allies and not their enemies.

The new Grinch toys are "sold out" in stores, but available direct from the manufacturer online.

Tired of working for someone else and getting paid what "they" feel you're worth?

By filling out this form you will "not enter" in to any obligations or contracts with us.

Transmissions to you by the sender of "this" email will be stopped promptly by sending an e-mail with REMOVE in the subject line.

"VERY CLEARLY" Print or Type.

Rather and **somewhat** are wimp words, affixed to strong words in an attempt to impart an air of reserve, as in *Salon these days seems to have been overrun by a bunch of rather extreme political viewpoints masquerading as objective journalism,* or to evade a commitment, as in *A lot of professional athletes are somewhat greedy. This is why we see strikes and lockouts every year.* To label something *somewhat exciting, rather severe, somewhat important,* or *rather dangerous* is to mute the loudest note in the sentence. A thing is either extreme or exciting or severe or important or dangerous or greedy or it is not.

Re- verbs are politically useful in a bureaucratic world. They do not imply creating something from scratch—a dangerous, independent proposition that carries hints of upper-level incompetence and radical action—but merely taking what already exists and modifying it into something new and wonderful.

Here are some of the most common new *re-* verbs and the words they have replaced, including older *re-* verbs.

reenergize, reinvigorate, revitalize	energize, improve, refresh, rejuvenate, restore

reengineer, reformulate, reinvent,	change, modify, remake,
repurpose, restructure	reorganize
regenerate	modify, revise, rework
relocate	move
rethink	reconsider, review

Re- verbs used fashionably are often also used incorrectly. *Mintel International believes Pepsi could re-invent [repeat] Gatorade's U.S. success in Europe.* Sometimes their meaning, despite the implied repeated action, is mysterious. *In his inaugural address, President Bush issued a call to reinvigorate citizenship.*

Reality has become a popular synonym for *the truth*, either by itself, as in *It's time we all faced reality*, or as an anchor for long-winded phrases.

A spokesperson for the industry noted that conflicting teenage tobacco usage data means we may never know the reality of the situation.

As with all trendy words, *reality* has had its meaning stretched far too broadly, giving it endless possible synonyms.

Can you follow simple step-by-step instructions and put forth the effort to make this a reality [happen] starting today?

Freedom of association, a right according to Mexican law and Nike's own code of conduct, is clearly not a reality at [permitted in] the Kuk-Dong factory.

While *reality* has been replacing *real*, *real* has been reduced to a synonym for *a lot of* in sentences such as *Would you like to make real money?*

See also MAJOR, MASSIVE, SERIOUS, SIGNIFICANT.

Reform is a noble-sounding word, like OPPORTUNITY, that has been forced into onerous service. As with many other CYNIC INCUBATORS, *reform* has a broad—and therefore useful—implied meaning: the changing of something bad into something good. Prisoners, corrupt institutions, and flawed legal systems can all be reformed.

Today, however, *reform* is frequently used when nothing more than change is what is happening. Market reforms, for example, do not necessarily result in a better economic system, but merely one that is different, i.e., more accommodating to the interests that demand them.

The roundabout way thrives in the worlds of commerce, government, and academia, where the ability to describe small concepts in oblique language is often rewarded. Advertising and PR have spread it to ordinary citizens, some of whom have picked it up as a cheap way to sound impressive, and the pestilence is now beyond control. The style hinders, rather than speeds, communication, but those who use it believe they sound better when they write or say *make a positive impact* for *help; in a bipartisan fashion* for *together; set forth in writing* for *written;* and *in the very near future* for *soon.*

Words for which the roundabout way is frequently substituted:

most
the bulk of, the majority of, the maximum number of

several, some, a few, many
some of the most, various (of the), a (wide) variety of/array of/assortment of, a number of, a period of

now, for now
in this day and age, at the present moment (in time), at this point (in time), in today's market, on an interim/ongoing/provisional basis

important, instrumental
a determining factor, a motivating factor, a dominant factor/issue, a key factor/issue, a major factor/issue, a key/major driver, a driving force

(By changing *a* to *the* in these examples one has the roundabout way to say *the cause* or *the reason*.)

Other examples, from the hundreds that are current:

in the near term	soon
on a case by case basis	individually
in short supply	scarce
fully functional/operational	working
on a positive note	happily
on a periodic basis	occasionally
a viable option	possible
a retail environment	a store
hypothetical scenario	guess

time restriction	deadline
primary concern	goal
skill set	skills
personal cash flow	spending habits
have a discussion	talk
begins promptly	starts
contact information	address, number, name
single point of reference	center
take it under consideration	think about it
the positive side of the equation	the good part
the political process	politics
the public sector	government
the private sector	business

See also BAD CONNECTIONS and OBESE PREPOSITIONS.

Run-on sentences are not bad because they are lengthy but because they are poorly written. Sentences ideally should contain a subject and a predicate, and express a complete thought. Sometimes that requires many words. Thoughtful writers choose and arrange their words with care, break them with punctuation to create rhythm, and strive for economy of expression even in sentences that must go on for some length.

English teachers everywhere discourage the use of run-on sentences. The following examples make it clear why they do.

Catalogs of our manufacturer's complete line of active wear included with your order including coupon entitling buyer to one free heart size custom digitized logo set up on any future order (manufacturer's expert digitizers will turn your logo into beautiful embroidery, a $200.00-$400.00 value free on any future order).

Mike Florio, The Utility Reform Network senior attorney, thought it was a bad idea but at the time had little clue that the $28 billion bailout would pale in comparison with the harm to consumers and the economy that resulted in 2000–2001 in the wake of a free market held captive by the new owners of generation plants that PG&E was forced to sell in the deregulation deal.

Your new e-mail pager has features like 50,000 character memory, message time stamping, automatic garbled message correction, beeps or vibrates, incandescent backlight, saved message folder, a unique never out of range feature that allows your pager to retrieve messages sent earlier when your pager was out of range or turned completely off.

Why the HCFA requirement for physician supervision of nurse anesthetists would be targeted for removal from the Medicare/Medicaid conditions of participations for hospitals and ambulatory centers has been questioned by members of the public and health care community throughout the three-year battle, Dr. Swissman noted.

This Gentle Ferocity Formulation is amalgamated in accordance with the fundamental Taoist herbal principle of botanical interactiveness and precursorship which in essence is a molecular equation of the relevant botanical/herbal alkaloids and glycosides interacting with one another to prolificate molecular communion and thereby to achieve demonstrative herbal efficaciousness without negative implication to any aspect of human composition.

The message was clear—passage of the Bush Administration's giant windfall-for-the-wealthy tax cut will reverse the Clinton-caused stock market slide and recession that's wiping out the retirement plans of middle income and working class Americans and turning the oil and energy cartel loose in the United States to extract more oil and gas and build more nuclear plants to produce an increasing "supply" of energy will ease Clinton-caused energy crisis.

Secondhand English. The misery of junk e-mail is occasionally relieved by assaults upon the American idiom that are too good to be blamed on translation software, too bad to be credited to a native English speaker. At least, one *hopes* that these sentences were written by people to whom English is unfamiliar.

Does such a store exist? Is it only in your wild imagination?

What it can be a problem or too much involvement of effort and time.

Come see what all the rave is about this Christmas!!

You get all what is needed for 99% of a small businesses, even for most big businesses, not to speak about personal use.

If hair loss is possibly a concern—This message is imperative!

Your phone number and email will not be sold or used in any manner but to comply with your request of us.

We will try to defect the user that send the scan and prevent this individual from do new illegal actions.

You'll be riveted to your computer screen! The software they're trying to ban! Before it's too late!

None of your days will be hum-drum. Your brain is Challenged.

Complete information system already developed, does the explaining for you!

Not like search engines or print ads that the potential customer has to do all the searching.

Click on the below link to be exclude from further communication.

Secret snob words are words and phrases, largely applied to people, that subtly convey class approval or disdain. *Elements*, for example, transforms objectionable people into something less than human: *undesirable elements* on our streets; *unruly elements* at our parades; *extremist elements* in our world. And the phrase *take issue with* is a signal that the challenging party is a member of a favored class. *Bush took issue with the claims raised by the newspaper report* but *The union representative denounced the counter-offer by DaimlerChrysler.*

The most prevalent secret snob word today is *professional.* The old days of *white collar worker* and *blue collar worker* are gone; we now have *workers* and *professionals,* and the class distinction is clear when one compares *business professionals* and *industry professionals* with *maintenance workers* and *garment workers.* There has been a drive of late among nonoffice groups to blur the distinction; *union workers* (or, worse, *laborers*) now call themselves *union professionals;* so do *health care workers.* As *professional* becomes more common, a new secret snob word will likely have to be created to replace it.

Curiously, *professional* was once the half-mocking term used to distinguish a prostitute from other women. It carried a message of class, however; a gentleman's escort might be a *professional,* but never a *whore.* And even today high-priced prostitutes sometimes refer to themselves as *sex professionals,* but never as *sex workers.*

Sector, in popular usage, serves as a substitute for *business* or *companies* or *industry,* particularly among those who think the word technical sounding and therefore impressive.

> The consumer long-distance sector is in decline.

> The market voiced its concerns about the automobile sector.

> Merrill Lynch analysts downgraded several companies within the fiber optic sector.

The real danger (and allure) of *sector,* as with most noun abstractions, is that it is a cornerstone for vague language.

> In eight years as Colorado's attorney general Norton refused to go after major polluters from the private sector [prosecute businesses that polluted heavily].

> During June the service sector continued to lead all industries in job creation. [Service companies created the most jobs in June.]

Self-deception helps make possible the effective manipulation of language by advertisers, PR writers, politicians, and other spin doctors with something to sell. It occurs when we feel a hope or desire that exceeds caution, a need to believe. It is self-deception that a salesperson counts on when he or she writes *only $19.95* and hopes you will think it a bargain, or when he or she says *virtually no cost* and hopes you will hear *free*. It makes possible, to varying degrees, the success of DISTRACTION MODIFIERS, EUPHEMISMS, INVISIBLE DIMINISHERS, and LACK OF WILL.

The darkest side of self-deception is the tendency to defend those whose goals are not in our best interests. This tendency exists perhaps because we have become a nation of salespeople, who must sell something to someone else—ourselves, our ideology, the products of our employer—to survive. When the product we buy or the politician we vote for or the dogma we embrace turns out to be, by any fair standard, unsatisfactory, we often do not get mad at those who sold us on them but at those who point out their inadequacy. We criticize the critics, branding them Cassandras or Jeremiahs or naysayers or dreambusters, or we dismiss them as CYNICAL or judgmental or NEGATIVE, as if they were the problem rather than the thing that failed to meet our expectations.

Self-help jargon is an odd mix of twelve-step lingo, New Age psychobabble, and hippie talk. In a time of business ascendency, when language has become hard-nosed and no-nonsense, it is odd that words and phrases such as *comfort level, quality time, closure, challenged, channeling, boundary issues, conflict resolution, identity crisis, internalize, validate, assertiveness, dysfunctional,* and *bonding* should be so prevalent. Self-help jargon is second only to BATTLE-FIELD LANGUAGE as a source of shop talk.

It is the self-help writers and consultants who have made it so, and the daytime talk shows and publishers and home-study industry that have given them a pulpit, and the would-be executives and politicians who read the books and take the courses and then appear on other shows to *externalize* and *engage in a dialogue* and tell us of *support* and *synergies, reality checks* and *modalities*. Duly impressed, we then disperse language in contexts where no self-help writers, consultants, professors, would-be executives, or politicians are present.

A solid handshake sets a confident aura about you from the first moment of contact.

Midwesterners have become enamored of the area and told Wilson that he, too, would easily find a comfort level working in New York.

Philip Morris has expanded its efforts to communicate more openly with the public.

Only Milo has the know-how to bring the project in on time, and he is seriously conflicted.

It's hard to verbalize what these new results really mean.

All of the ingredients work synergistically to renew that showroom, new car look.

The company strives to enable more people to research and locate mortgage information.

An excerpt from a job application letter shows just how far afield this kind of stuff can go.

> I decided to apply for this position because I realized that I needed to accept my challenge and do something positive to achieve growth.

Situation, an abstract noun, is used as a EUPHEMISM for the concrete noun *problem* or as an evasive or lazy substitute for describing a particular kind of problem. In those roles it is a near-perfect synonym of ISSUE and, in some cases, *concerns* and *challenges*.

> The spouse-batterer needs treatment. This won't happen unless the situation is reported.

> We are hopeful that as the system runs its course, the situation will be resolved positively.

> It would not be appropriate for us to comment on the situation.

> Thank you for writing to Tripod regarding this situation.

> "All we're trying to do is make the cash-flow situation a situation that we can handle," Colangelo explained.

> Exports will be tied to the human rights situation in China.

> Since the issue resides on one of our foreign servers, we cannot immediately impact this situation.

> "There is no situation," McClendon snapped when pressed on the issue.

Sloppy Metaphors. A young woman tells her forgetful spouse to *stop using me as your hard drive* and instantly gets her point across; a newspaper article reports on a nursing home's *warehousing of the elderly* and paints a nasty picture in one's mind; a cell phone plan advertisement promises *the freedom to talk your face off* and vividly conveys its point.

Simple metaphorical words and phrases are so abundant that they are barely noticeable. Newspapers are filled with *incubator* companies, *emerging* technologies, *nailing* a deal, *building* a business, *launching* a Web site, *multifaceted* investment strategies, *niche* marketing, *solid* numbers, and of various *engines* that are *fueling* or *driving* or, more accurately, *powering* the economy. A complex metaphor, however, is more difficult to craft, and when it is botched it does not breathe life into an idea, but kills the thought it was intended to convey.

> The platforms on which the candidates ran were as calculated and artificial as plastic topiary.

> He would have been a solid anchor on a team that slipped into a rebuilding mode last season.

> The aura of the five-ring Olympic logo has obscured the negative environmental fallout from the games in recent years.

> The Chicago Cubs appear to be one of many teams perched upon the Gary Sheffield rumor mill.

> The comet-struck electric disintegration in the last few weeks are the embers of a decade of money grubbing.

Nowhere on earth can a nation survive if it is totally burdened by the parasites who live only to eat away at the foundations of decency.

The obviously bright but terminally arrogant Vice President flashed his brittle core and lost an election that had been handed to him on a silver platter.

Smears. Each generation creates new names for its villains. A hundred years ago the world had *anarchists,* followed by *agitators, subversives, leftists, radicals, militants,* and most recently *racists, fanatics,* and *terrorists.* Words such as these are tools of propaganda, designed to stir hatred, not promote thinking. One person's *terrorist* is another's *freedom fighter;* a *racist* to one is a *champion of* (name your color or ethnic group) *nationalism* to another.

Currently the most creative hate language in our culture is directed not at other nations or ethnic or religious groups but at people who challenge laissez-faire capitalism. Added to the all-purpose *cynic* and *doomsayer* and *liberal*—the latter, like *conservative,* ruined by politics—are inventions such as *ecoterrorist* for the person who opposes logging; *e-commerce terrorist* and the old, but newly applied, *sociopath* for one who disrupts on-line business; *anti-commerce radicals* for those who oppose telemarketing; *animal protection extremists* for those who protest product testing on dogs and rabbits; and *dreambusters* for those who question the claims of self-help financial hucksters.

Social Welfare Lingo. *We work with partners in the business world who also strive to recognize and honor the diversity of gifts and* *perspectives in our global community.* So reads a flyer, written by a PR copywriter, found in a toothpaste box.

Social welfare lingo is as self-serving as any other that exists only to cast a favorable light on the viewpoint of a particular group. It has its own set of EUPHEMISMS, all politically correct, some more accepted than others: *drug addicts* are *substance abusers, jails* are *correctional facilities, the lower class* is *disadvantaged, the poor* are *high-need, the retarded* are *mentally challenged* or *learning-impaired.* But it is a real stretch when a business co-opts social welfare lingo—*empower, diversity, celebration, community, people of color, wellness, human spirit, struggle, pride, multicultural, positive experience, making a difference*—to portray itself as socially responsible, as does the flyer quoted above when it speaks of sending a *Consumer Dialogue representative,* likely an employee of the same PR firm that wrote it, to local grade schools to make *meaningful connections* with eight-year-olds.

Solutions. The days when *solutions* was synonymous with *answers* are gone. Today *solutions* are anything that a person can be persuaded to buy.

AT&T has streamlined the process of bringing customized business solutions [products] to market.

We are certain that we will be able to provide top of the class solution [product] packages to our clients in the Asia Pacific region.

You'll receive the innovative solutions [products] you need to help you reach your financial goals.

One could say that solutions are a special class of products, different from, for example, coffee or toasters, which are products that do not solve anything. But coffee, in fact, is the solution to the early-morning energy-beverage problem, and toasters are the solution to the controlled carbonization of bread problem. The trick is to define as a *problem* the part of life that your product alters; once you do that you can call your product a *solution* and you are in business.

Space has recently appeared as an awkward synonym for what we used to call *field*, *area*, or *market*.

> We provide you with critical, decision-making information that aids the chance of investment success in this lucrative space.

> Your information will only be shared with companies that are in the life sciences space and pass our rigorous inspection.

Those who abuse *space* in this way should be aware that the word is also synonymous with *void*.

Speak No Evil. People placed on the spot—usually corporate mouthpieces and politicians—have long adhered to the approach that the less said that is unpleasant, the better. A witness testifying at John Tower's unsuccessful confirmation hearing referred gingerly to his frequent "condition of nonsobriety." President Clinton described the politically indefensible murder of at least a half-million Rwandans with the sentence, "Acts of genocide may have occurred." In the mid-1960s, Robert McNamara, secretary of defense, defined killing in Vietnam as "autocratic methods within a democratic framework." And sometimes the need to avoid saying disagreeable things makes a spokesperson so mealy-mouthed that he or she must recast axioms to pull it off.

> "We're not in the business of running investigations,"
> Phillips said. "We have a system that passes judgment. We're in
> a situation that you're innocent until it is otherwise determined."

EUPHEMISMS are the stock in trade of those who speak no evil. Some of the most common include *disparity* for *inequality; indiscretion* or *mishap* for *mistake; adverse effect* for *injury, harm, damage,* or *death;* ISSUE, SITUATION, and *difficulty* for *problem; challenge,* which also replaces *problem* and then puts a positive spin on it; *concern,* which replaces *problem, fear, worry,* and *danger;* and NEGATIVE, which, while it does not disguise badness, is much less bad than the words it replaces. The strong words *dishonest, fraud, crimes,* and *selfish* have nearly vanished from our vocabulary, replaced by *unethical, irregularities, misdeeds,* and the empty terms *egocentric, self-centered, self-serving,* and *self-directed.*

> Heading into the tail end of a bull year, there are few
> analysts who do not believe a potentially devastating correction
> [collapse] is inevitable.

> In November the vice president had a strong and
> prolonged—about an hour—episode of chest discomfort [pain].

> Fiscal irresponsibility could fuel recession fears and plunge
> the Western region and, ultimately, the country into further
> economic uncertainty [crisis].

Softening one's language out of a desire to spare those who are distraught or suffering, or even as a courtesy to a friend, is an act of kindness and civility; we would be less than human if we did not occasionally enlist EUPHEMISMS and circumlocution to express uncomfortable or offensive ideas tactfully. But those who routinely use print and electronic media to speak no evil to us are not trying to spare our feelings. *Adverse effects*, unlike *injuries*, do not move us to action, and *issues* and *situations* do not cry out to be solved.

Strung-Together Nouns. To use a noun as an adjective—what is called in grammar an attributive noun—is common in English. Examples abound in everyday speech—*screen* door, *nursery* school. But to line up a series of nouns as attributes, all leaning on one another like books on a lightly stocked shelf, can confuse the reader as to what exactly is modifying what.

Strung-together nouns can be unstrung by restoring the articles and prepositions—the *of*s, *in*s, *the*s, *from*s, and *for*s—that were removed to make them. Thus *focus group feedback analysis methodologies* becomes *methods for analyzing the feedback from focus groups*—far from perfect, but better than it was.

Stuffing occurs when multiple (and possibly even conflicting) meanings are assigned to a single word or phrase that does not intrinsically carry any exact connotations. To write *family values* when what is meant is *beliefs approved by conservative Christians* is to stuff two simple words with a meaning they don't necessarily have. This is willful deception—the use of stuffing as a camouflage to hide words that the writer wishes to avoid.

Stuffing is usually deliberate, as when advertisers or politicians or PR front groups use agreeably vague terms such as *deregulate* and *market reform*, or applaud something with CYNIC INCUBATORS such as *progress* and *freedom*, or damn it with SMEARS such as *radical* and *reckless*, without getting into specifics.

Concise words fall into disuse at the expense of broad, general terms, which are stuffed so full of meaning that they no longer mean anything; a QUALITY book, for example, may be well written and full of insight, or it may simply have a nice binding.

System. Any product described as a *system* that is not composed of ducts, pipes, or electrical components—e.g., *hair-growth system, bust-development system, weight-loss system, stock-investing system, e-mail–marketing system*—is a fraud.

Team Sports Terminology. The influx of team sports terminology into idiomatic English has resulted in the near elimination of certain words from some people's vocabularies. *Goal* has nearly expelled *intent, object, end, aim*, and *ambition* from common usage; *time-out* has replaced *break* (*let's take a time-out*) and, as a command, *stop* (*Time-out!*); we speak informally of *teamwork*, not *cooperation*, in our marriages and families; we tell those who fail to meet our standards that they did not *make the cut*; we plead for fairness by asking for *a level playing field*; and a passionate encounter is still a *score* to many men. We have also formed dozens of CLICHÉS and idiomatic expressions from the world of sports in general: *jockeying for position, toeing the line, hitting below the belt*, etc.

Tech Talk will flourish as long as machinery and science are equated with status. While it may sound more impressive to *calculate a response* than to *guess* it, the coldness and artificiality of tech talk make it a poor alternative to the plain words it replaces. It is simply not natural to use *feedback* for *opinion, synthesis* for *combination, components* and *elements* for *parts, tabulations* for *sums*, and *methodology* instead of *approach*.

To activate the record function, depress the P and R buttons simultaneously.

Word power mastery is an essential component of a successful career.

If DeWine really wanted a balanced exploration of the problem he would have asked for some input from union members.

In the early years he would go to local schools and interface with students.

"I think there's some methodology in my travels," Bush said.

Technology. As a nation of pragmatists, we like to believe that nearly any problem can be solved by building a better mousetrap. Thus the word *technology* will always have a special place in our hearts, and any advertising or PR copywriter worth his or her paycheck will go to great lengths to place the word in close proximity to his or her product: *auto-repair technology, food-processing technology, a breakthrough learning technology,* etc. Although *technology* calls to mind images of scientific research, products graced with it may or may not fit that description.

Isotonic memory foam is the latest in sleeping technology.

We are about to offer a major advancement in Tooth Whitening Technology!

C-ESTA Cleansing Gel containing DAE Complex is a newly developed cleansing technology that compliments the use of C-ESTA facial products.

Purina—Corporate leader in pet food technology.

Reliv Skin Technology is based on a unique compound found only in the avocado.

By real-time monitoring of nutrition levels in the blood, "Just in Time" eating technology prolongs life expectancy four-fold; you just need to be a little flexible, that's all.

Rockport applies the latest walking technology to their unique comfort design.

Our sales staff is highly trained in new carpet technology and understands how new carpet products offer unique solutions for home and office.

We have become so used to seeing *technology* set to work in this agreeably inexact way that it has assumed a power unto itself, like QUALITY and VALUE, and has become popular with writers who realize that an artfully positioned *technology* is the best they can offer to an otherwise unimpressive subject.

Students can trace social history, which is closely related to political history, through the evolution of eating technology.

Terminate. We are losing the ability to admit that something is simply *over.* A theatrical production *ends*, and television shows are still *canceled*, but products and services never are; they are *discontinued*, or, now, worse, they are *terminated*. Advertising and PR copywriters were the first to employ the word, as in *We reserve the right to terminate the frequent flyer program, thus terminating* *your ability to claim rewards.* But it has become trendy, other writers have adopted it, and sentences such as the following are no longer unusual.

> The account responsible has been located and terminated.
>
> There are guidelines when it comes to termination of service.
>
> Termination is a business procedure just like hiring.
>
> A recent Court of Appeals decision allowed a terminated employee to sue his supervisor.

Tiny Type Messages. After all the bluster and selling, at the bottom of a page filled with bold, large type in pretty colors—is the truth. It is in tiny type, sometimes in print so pale as to be barely readable, always positioned where we are least likely to look.

Actual results may vary.

Additional terms and conditions may apply.

Advance reservations are required.

Annual percentage rate may vary.

Any testimonials or amounts of earnings listed in this letter
    may be factual or fictitious.

Blackout dates may apply.

Certain restrictions, limitations, and exclusions apply.

Chart for comparison only.

Limit one coupon per customer.

Limit one per household.

May not be available in all areas.

May not be used in combination with any other offer.

Not all parts are covered.

Not valid with any other offer or promotion.

Offer may be modified or withdrawn at any time without prior notice.

Other fees may apply.

Prices subject to change without notice.

Products may vary in appearance from those pictured.

Rates, terms, and conditions may vary.

Results may vary.

Shipping and handling charges are extra.

Some of the above newsletters were compensated for writing about the company.

Some restrictions apply.

Subject to availability.

Subject to government approval.

Terms and conditions are subject to change.

We reserve the right to change program rules, regulations, awards, and special offers at any time without notice.

You can telephone us, but doing so will not preserve your rights.

Transparent. The current vogue for *transparent* as a fashionable metaphor has left little use for *clear* and for many more specific words that are not figures of speech: *candid, straightforward, frank, direct, open, simple, obvious, plain, understandable.* The appearance of *transparent*—a word meant to describe the clearness of physical objects—in sentences about abstract concepts, like law and estimates, often results in a expressions that are, ironically, unclear.

This finding is the first transparent estimate of the quantities of antibiotics used in meat production.

The company expects that the settlement will help build a more talented workforce by bringing total transparency to how employees are hired, paid, promoted, and evaluated.

The network of Freedom of Information Acts and sunshine laws enacted by the federal and state governments in the past generation are supposed to make the workings of government transparent.

The more transparent a prison is, the healthier it is.

Unique, a word that means one of a kind, is freely bandied about by advertising copywriters and others who wish to imbue whatever position or product or person they wish to sell with a certain high status. That so few things really are unique is precisely what gives the word its power. *Unique*'s veracity has been shaved away by phrases such as *practically unique, virtually unique, somewhat unique, most unique*, and so on, which, truthfully, mean *not* unique.

This is not to say that the products or positions or people being touted are not notable, special, exceptional, fabulous, marvelous, worthy, or rare, but it is highly unlikely that they are in fact *unique*.

Unique has been stretched so thin through misuse that it has become invisible, a CHEAPENED WORD, and the copywriter who used it in the sentence *In this catalog you'll find unique products that you won't find anywhere else* was probably in earnest.

Useless cabooses are words added to the ends of sentences by writers who seem unwilling to let go, perhaps unsure that what they have written is enough to convey their idea. *We may be unable to extend credit if, after you respond to this offer, we determine* *that you no longer meet our applicable criteria bearing on creditworthi-ness that we have established.* The writer could have quit after the word *criteria* with no loss of (if not a clearer sense of) meaning.

Useless cabooses are particularly irritating since, unlike THE ROUNDABOUT WAY, they are not overlong ways of expressing thoughts but either are redundant or add no meaning.

The press seem to swarm like a hive to these announcements once or twice a year *on a regular basis these days.*

They are now restricting the right of investors to request a review *at all.*

The signing of Johnson would hardly make a dent in their payroll *structure.*

I didn't have much choice *in the matter.*

Singer also sold abroad, arguably becoming the first multi-national corporation *in the process.*

There is no need to modify our existing policy *as such.*

We will continue to presenting the cutting edge of cinema *on an ongoing basis.*

In times of prosperity banks are willing to make riskier loans *than under normal circumstances.*

Please complete this form *with the requested information.*

The site has been redesigned to make navigation more flexible *from a user perspective.*

We offer an array of financial services *products.*

Value is used in contexts in which its only apparent purpose is to cover plain English with a slippery gloss of obsequiousness.

We value your input.

We value the relationship we have built with you and your continued business is important to us.

These gifts are available at discount prices only to our most valued customers.

He is a valued friend.

Warfare English. Those who deceive the public for profit have a dark side, but they shine with angelic radiance compared to those who manipulate the language to hide responsibility for the murder, rape, and torture of other human beings.

War has always been difficult to sell. It has become as much a battle of public relations as of ideology or trade and has enlisted its own troops of diversionary EUPHEMISMS to allow politicians to hide behind semantic or legalistic distinctions; the *police action* of Korea is the first modern example. World War II is fondly regarded as our country's last "good" war, in part because in those days the government was still willing to call a spade a spade, no matter how horrific that might be. In 1943 Admiral William F. Halsey erected a billboard with the very unambiguous message KILL JAPS, KILL JAPS, KILL MORE JAPS; today America's leaders still send troops to kill, but they rely on a bureaucratic miasma of words to hide the ugly truth.

What was, until 1949, the *Department of War* is now the *Department of Defense*, and it is perhaps only a matter of time before it becomes the Orwellian *Department of Peace*. The United States, while instigating such actions as Operation Desert Storm (the invasion of Iraq) and Operation Just Cause (the invasion of

Panama), has not issued an official declaration of war (including the Vietnam War) since the reorganization of the Department of War into the Department of Defense.

Of the following current military-political euphemisms employed by our government, *friendly fire* is perhaps the best known and accepted.

act of aggression = attack

administered areas = captured lands

antiresistance measures = armed suppression

armed conflict = war

armed intervention = war

armed resistance = terrorism

barbarian; heathen; pagan = the religious beliefs of one's enemy

casualties = wounded or dead people

civil patrols; insurgents; irregular forces; militias; paramilitary groups; security forces = armed groups that commit murder and terrorism for a government while providing deniability for the government and its armed forces

collateral damage = wounded or dead civilians

compulsory labor = enslavement

covert action = terrorism

detainees = prisoners, hostages

disappeared = to be arrested secretly, with torture and murder implied

disinformation = lies

displaced persons = refugees

extrajudicial execution = murder

firm measures = killing

forced labor = enslavement

freedom fighters = terrorists

friendly fire = being shot at by your own troops

incursion = invasion

insurrection = revolution

internal matter = civil war

internment camp = concentration camp

a military solution = war

monitoring devices = spy equipment

occupied territories = captured lands

ordnance = bombs

pacification = annihilation, slaughter

plausible deniability = legally acceptable lies

police action = war

reeducation = indoctrination, usually under physical and mental duress

security measures = punishment, marshal law

soft ordnance = napalm

subversives = citizens whose political beliefs differ from those who rule

surveillance = spying

suspected area = minefield

transit camp = concentration camp

traumatic amputation = having an arm or leg blown off

uprising = war

use of force = war

war of liberation = revolution

war of self-determination = revolution

work obligation = enslavement